Face to Face Skills

A practical guide to interactive skills

Peter Honey

Gower

First published as *Face to Face* 1976 by Institute of Personnel Management

Second edition published 1988 by Gower Publishing Company Limited

This paperback edition published 1990 by Gower Publishing Company Limited,
Gower House,
Croft Road,
Aldershot,
Hampshire GU11 3HR, ·
England

Gower Publishing Company
Old Post Road
Brookfield
Vermont 05036
U.S.A.

British Library Cataloguing in Publication Data
Honey, Peter
    Face to face skills: a practical guide to interactive skills
    1. Communication in management
    2. Interpersonal communication
    I. Title
    302.3′36′024658   HD30.3

ISBN 0 566 02873 5

Printed in Great Britain by
Billing & Sons Ltd, Worcester

Contents

Preface

This book is about behaviour in face to face encounters or interactions. It argues that behaviour is critical in human relationships precisely because it is the bit of us that is readily evident to other people. Their attitudes towards us and, more importantly, their *behaviour* towards us are determined largely by our behaviour towards them. This interaction between people's behaviour is important because it affects what is achieved or not achieved. This means that each of us has behavioural responsibilities; and interactive skills are concerned with meeting those responsibilities through being thoughtful and thus consciously employing certain behaviours in certain situations.

In many ways the interactive skills approach, in common with other approaches that seek to help people to modify their behaviour, makes unpalatable demands on us. It demands specificity rather than ambiguity, discipline rather than disorder, conscious control rather than spontaneity. It also assumes that interactive skills, unrelieved by gimmicks or golden rules, have to be learned and worked at continuously lest we fall into unthinking modes of behaviour. Initially, this may seem an unnatural struggle but, as with the acquisition of *any* skill, with practice the skills become absorbed as an unobtrusive part of us. When you are learning to ride a bicycle it is faster to walk: when you are learning to think about behaviour it is easier not to!

Any approach that acknowledges the influence of behaviour is bound to arouse ethical concerns. For the most part these concerns are healthy and help to safeguard us against manipulative practices. Often, however, these concerns lead to an ostrich-like refusal to recognize behaviour as an influential factor at all or to the absurd claim that all that matters is that your behaviour should be an accurate reflection of your underlying feelings. Is it unethical to admit to trying to control behaviour so that it is appropriate to the circumstances of a situation? It depends when and how it is done of course and this is precisely the line taken by an interactive skills approach: that there is a time and a place for every behaviour and that the crucial skill is deciding when and where. This book unashamedly encourages you to practise the skills involved in arranging your behaviour so that it is 'in step' with objectives and the circumstances of the situation. It does so believing that we desperately need to learn to interact more competently in all our encounters whether at work or at home.

Interactive skills, and behavioural approaches in general, are often criticized as being manipulative. Naturally, this point is taken up at intervals throughout the text but suffice at this stage to say that manipulation involves being furtive, clandestine and ambiguous. Interactive skills, on the other hand, involve being open and explicit. Objectives, for example, cannot be shared between people unless they are in a form capable of articulation. Similarly, things cannot be fruitfully agreed, or disagreed for that matter, unless specific communication skills are employed: trust cannot grow unless there is sufficient match between what is said and what is done, and so on. Interactive skills, like any other skills, are amoral. They can be used for the forces of good or for the forces of evil. You can use your skills to sell a good product or an inadequate one, to persuade people to a proper or improper course of action, to help people subscribe to mutually advantageous objectives or to trick them into subscribing to selfish one-sided ones. One of the best safeguards against the misuse of interactive skills is to have as many people as possible actively employing the five basic skills described later. The more skilful and behaviourally competent we are, the less likely it is that we shall fall prey to manipulative practices either as a consumer or a purveyor.

The preceding paragraphs appeared in the preface to the first edition of this book. In the ten years or so since then, interactive skills have become more widely accepted as a set of legitimate and learnable skills. My impression is that it is now easier to convince people that their behavioural style is more made than born, and that they can, if they wish, choose how to behave in their face to face dealings with people. The old pessimistic arguments that behaviour is instinctive and that a leopard cannot change its spots are heard less often.

Also I detect much more willingness to acknowledge that the way people behave in their dealings with other people is often *the* deciding factor. This is especially true in customer dealings where many businesses have realized that the quality of the interface between them and their customers is as important as the quality of their products.

Ten years ago I was almost apologetic about using the word 'behaviour'. Now it can be used unashamedly without people bracing themselves for something 'odd' or accusing me of using jargon. This is not to suggest that interactive skills have 'arrived', in the sense that people are significantly more skilful than they were a decade ago. I do, however, maintain that the general level of behavioural awareness is much higher. Awareness is a prerequisite for change though not, alas, a sufficient condition to ensure it. Awareness plus skills is the recipe that does the trick. This book aims to help on both counts; to raise your awareness about behavioural matters and to show you how to further develop your interactive skills.

I have made a number of changes to the original text, the most important of which are some modifications to the behaviour categories introduced in Chapter 5; a complete update of Chapter 7 in the light of my research into the effects certain behaviours have on people's reactions; and the addition of a new chapter on non-verbal behaviour (Chapter 8).

Peter Honey

1 Introducing behaviour

The main emphasis throughout this book is on the practice, rather than the theory, of interactive skills. You may feel that the very expression 'interactive skills' belies this claim immediately, but I hope to make you easily and quickly familiar with a few pieces of what you could call jargon.

Initially we can say that interactive skills are the skills you or I use in face to face encounters to arrange our behaviour so that it is in step with our objectives. This means that interactive skills have very little to do with being nice or winning friends, unless those sorts of outcomes are encapsulated in the objectives. The whole idea is to see how successful we can be at using our behaviour to increase the probability of achieving our objectives. Our behaviour is a means that can, depending on our skill, either help or hinder us in achieving our ends.

Before we explore the various techniques in subsequent chapters, it is important to agree on a few basics. I have already used the word behaviour, for example, so what does that actually refer to? Even more fundamental is the whole issue of whether behaviour matters anyway. Does the way we behave during an interaction really make a significant difference to the outcome? Even if it does, where does it come in the league table of influential factors? Is it just an 'optional extra' or is our behaviour an essential ingredient? Does it *always* matter or are there interactive situations where it is appropriate to 'freewheel' and not consciously concern ourselves with behavioural issues?

These and questions like them are the primary concern of this first chapter.

BEHAVIOUR DEFINED

First, what do I mean by behaviour? The word is not exactly a piece of jargon but that is precisely its danger. At least if a word strikes us as jargon it is likely to provoke a query as to its meaning. The word behaviour is one with which we are all familiar. Indeed, most people associate it particularly with childhood where warnings about the need to behave properly were prevalent!

'Behaviour' refers, quite simply, to everything we do which is overt or observable. It therefore embraces an enormous range; reflexes like our leg jerking when the muscles are hit in a certain position or like the pupils of our eyes contracting and expanding under different light conditions; all sorts of learned habits like riding a bicycle, tying shoe laces, nodding approval when people say something we agree with: the whole gamut of verbal and non-verbal actions and reactions of which we are capable.

The range is so great that I shall cream off the behaviour we use in interactive situations for primary attention in this book. Accordingly, we shall not be paying attention to muscular reflexes or to what are known as 'motor' habits (walking, swimming, driving a car, etc) because they are not very significant in face to face interactions between people. Our concern is with what are variously called interpersonal, social or communicating behaviour: the words we speak to make our point; the intonation we use; the accompanying non-verbal behaviour such as facial expressions, gestures with our hands and the bodily posture we adopt (referred to, quite literally, by many researchers as our body *language*).

The main point to grasp is that behaviour is *always* directly observable. This may seem a trite point to be starting with but the implications are considerable. For example, I shall argue that one of the reasons our behaviour is important is precisely because it is so immediately visible to others. The people we interact with can *see* our facial expressions and they can *hear* our words. The conclusions they reach about us are primarily based on this visible behaviour. The conclusions we reach about them are based, quite naturally, on our observations of their behaviour. In a sense, our behaviour is all we have got going for us in our face to face dealings with people.

A further implication which we shall explore in much more detail is that because our behaviour quite literally 'shows' it has a direct impact on the behaviour we get back from other people. I shall illustrate later how behaviour is infectious (you yawn they yawn, you smile they smile and so on). I shall also show how it is possible to influence the reactions of others by using your own behaviour to 'shape' theirs.

DISTINCTION BETWEEN BEHAVIOUR, ATTITUDES, EMOTIONS AND OTHER UNDERLYING FACTORS

If we define behaviour as all we do that is overt, doesn't that leave a lot unsaid? Is this too superficial a definition? What about important things like attitudes, feelings and motives? Surely our behaviour, when all is said and done, is only the tip of an iceberg?

I am not suggesting that our behaviour is *all* there is to us, merely that it is the most *visible* aspect — just like the tip of an iceberg in fact. Beneath our behavioural surface lurk all sorts of enormously complicated underlying factors, so complicated that behavioural scientists are nowhere near to unravelling all the variables and explaining why people behave as they do. In broad terms our behaviour is the visible output resulting from the interpretations we make about the world about us. We are always operating within an external environment of some kind and our senses are continually at work absorbing information about our surroundings. There is too much for us consciously to pay attention to everything and so we operate a number of filters. We pay close attention to, say, the people in our meeting, keep half an eye on the clock on the wall and pay no attention to the distant noise of passing traffic. As soon as something fairly dramatic happens we switch our attention, if only momentarily, to that: a 'plane flies over, a secretary arrives with coffee, the room gets too hot and so on.

All this information goes, via our senses, into a sort of central processor where it is sorted, interpreted and given meaning. This is a remarkable process which is unique to each person. It seems that our past experience in sifting all the incoming information leaves a residue of learning. The conclusions we have reached in the past contaminate, to a greater or lesser extent, our future interpretations. If we concluded that so and so was a fuddy duddy last time we had dealings with him it will certainly predispose us to view him in that light again. Our attitude towards him is important because, unless we deliberately control our behaviour, it will affect the overt reactions we display towards him. That may or may not matter, of course, depending on our relationship with him and on our purposes for the interaction with him.

The residue we accrue from handling millions of pieces of information in our central processor combines together to result in our capabilities (what we can do and can't do) on the one hand, and our inclinations (what we want to do and don't want to do) on the other. The knowledge and skills we acquire through formal and informal learning are two important factors that play a part in determining our capabilities, for example. On the other hand, our attitudes, feelings, temperament or moods, our motives and interests are examples of the sorts of factors that influence our inclinations.

I shall not dwell on these underlying factors to any great extent because, important though they are in helping us to understand the totality of our personal make-up, they are not primarily what this book is about. We are concerned with the skills involved in arranging manifest behaviour so that it is appropriate to objectives and the circumstances of the situations in which we find ourselves. The emphasis is therefore, quite properly, going to be on behaviour itself: on what goes on between people above the behavioural surface.

Largely to disregard the interplay between underlying factors such as knowledge, skills, attitudes and emotions is not as superficial as it might at first appear. There is plenty of evidence to suggest that these sorts of beneath the surface factors do not enjoy a monopoly in determining why people behave as they do. Why is it, for example, that if you smile at people, not inanely but nevertheless fairly frequently, it has the effect of 'causing' them to increase their smiling rate significantly? Why is it, to use another simple non-verbal example, that if you nod your head while people are talking to you it 'causes' them to talk for longer than if you keep your head still?

These examples serve to remind us that our behaviour, visible and manifest, often has a fairly direct influence on the behaviour of others or vice versa. It is true that *all* observations of behaviour go through the central processor before an output, such as a return reaction, appears. But the point is that much behaviour can be satisfactorily explained at a behavioural level, and it is not always necessary for us to have recourse to underlying factors either to understand behaviour or to change it.

The advantage of this emphasis on visible behaviour itself is that we do not need to become amateur, or even professional, psychologists before we can be successful in our interactions with people as managers, salesmen, politicians or personnel specialists. We *do* need to become good at basic skills such as observing behaviour accurately, arranging our own behaviour appropriately and controlling our behaviour accordingly. It is these basic skills that this book is about.

When I advance these arguments people often ask 'But surely we must take people's attitudes and feelings into account when we interact with them?' My answer is that of course it is important to have empathy for the feelings of others. In doing so, we must recognize that inferring the presence or otherwise of certain motives, feelings and attitudes in others will always have to be speculative. This is because the underlying factors are invisible. You cannot have direct access to the attitudes of others, nor to their emotions nor, for that matter, to their skills, knowledge and intelligence. The best you can do is to observe their behaviour and, working backwards from that, 'guess' about the presence or absence of these things. Once again, we see that behaviour itself is different in kind from the underlying factors. Behaviour is visible; underlying factors are invisible.

Behaviour emerges again as an attribute of especial importance. You may like someone very much and find them a pleasure to do business with but, unless you behave as if you do, they will never know. Conversely you may be utterly bored by your interactions with someone and wish that they wouldn't be so long winded but unless you 'behave it' they cannot know. In a very real sense this is why the behavioural sciences tend to emphasize the importance of openness, explicitness and candour between people. It stems from the realization that relationships depend on how people behave in the face to face dealings they have with one another. Extremely shy or introverted people are handicapped in the sense that they frequently fail to generate enough explicit behaviour. They tend to 'sell other people short' behaviourally and therefore to leave them uncomfortable about the interaction. How often have you been left guessing about whether so and so was quiet because he agreed with everything and was therefore content to acquiesce silently? Or because he was bored and not listening? Or because he disapproved but didn't like to say so? Your interpretations have to be based on the behaviour you observed. If you are left short of behaviour then the more you are left guessing.

Many practices that we take for granted stem from this basic distinction between behaviour itself and underlying factors. For example, because it is not possible to know what someone *feels* about his work, ways and means have been devised to get people to *say* what they feel. Attitude surveys, questionnaires and interviews all have this basic aim. Once someone has been encouraged to articulate his feelings, some behaviour has been provoked that can be listened to, absorbed, probed further and so on. Examinations were invented with similar basic aims. Since it is not possible to know whether someone knows something or not, he or she has to be stimulated into overtly demonstrating whether they knew it by, for example, answering an examination question or, in practical exams, by physically demonstrating that they possess the knowledge (and skills perhaps). People who are not able to behave well in examination conditions suffer badly because judgements about the extent of their knowledge are indirectly based on the overt behaviour itself. Once again behaviour is shown to be a crucial factor. At best you can only guess about other people's underlying factors. Their behaviour you can be quite certain about.

BEHAVIOUR AND PERSONALITY

Perhaps it would be helpful to clear up another basic confusion that worries people when highlighting the distinction between behaviour and other associated variables. The query that often comes up is about the relationship between personality and behaviour. Are they the same? If not, what is the difference and is it of any importance?

Using an analogy seems the simplest way in which to draw the distinction between personality and behaviour. Imagine you are a goat in a field. You are tethered by a rope to a stake that has been driven into the ground and is steadfast. The position of the stake in the field and the length of the rope quite naturally determine the area you can roam. Strain as you might they set limits on your freedom. There are parts of the field you cannot get to. On the other hand, providing your tether is not cruelly short, you have plenty of room for manoeuvre with the stake as a central point. Let us call the circumference around the stake your personality. In other words your personality sets boundaries beyond which you can't go. No-one is quite agreed on a totally satisfactory definition of personality but there is a consensus that it is a global term summing up all the ingredients that we have already mentioned as capabilities and inclinations. Your personality is, if you like, the thread of consistency that runs through everything you do. The consistencies are considerable even though it is popular to claim that people are largely unpredictable. When you claim to *know* someone well, for example, what that actually means is that you have sampled their behaviour sufficiently to say that you feel fairly confident about predicting how they will behave in the future. Even inconsistent people are consistently inconsistent!

So personality is an umbrella term summing up our totality. Part of us, as we have already seen, can be singled out for special attention and called our behaviour. The relationship between the two is now clear. Personality sets the constraints or boundaries but within it we are able to behave in various ways and even, if we wish, to make considerable modifications to our behaviour. Personality, by the time we are adults and probably much earlier, is relatively fixed and unchanging. Our overt behaviour, however, is amenable to a process of continual modification and change. Personality can change when something really dramatic intervenes: the equivalent of pulling up the goat's stake and driving it into the ground in another field altogether. Brainwashing, certain drugs and brain damage can alter the threads of consistency running through someone's behaviour. Short of such drastic happenings we are free within the confines set by our personalities to experiment with our behaviour.

Most people do not do so, however. In fact researchers show time and time again that most of us are stuck in well-worn behavioural ruts. Even though we may *claim* to adapt our behaviour to changing circumstances, people and situations that we encounter, most of us fail to use anything like the full range of behavioural options that our personalities leave open to us.

It is rather like the goat always grazing close to the stake and never moving out to the extremities, or like the goat only grazing, say, a 90 degree segment and leaving the other three quarters unexplored.

One of the hallmarks of an interactively skilled person is that he or she has a behavioural repertoire which is wide enough to give them genuine choice in deciding how best to behave in differing situations. Sometimes they hog it and do most of the talking. At other times they sit back and listen. Sometimes they produce lots of ideas. At others they hold back their own ideas and tease suggestions out of other people. Sometimes they choose to behave with absolute certainty and at other times to behave hesitantly, and so on.

DOES BEHAVIOUR MATTER?

So far I hope to have shown you that behaviour is always overt and therefore directly observable and that, unless they are directly translated into behaviour, underlying attitudes, emotions and so on are invisible. We have also looked at the relationship between overt behaviour and the total compass of personality itself. That leaves the question: does the way we behave in face to face interactions with people actually matter? To what extent is behaviour an influential factor in determining the outcome of our interactions?

In so far as we have already established that people's judgements about us stem from their observations of our behaviour it would seem to be clear that our behaviour matters very much.

Certainly whenever we are in situations where we wish to impress or to gain personal credibility our behaviour is absolutely crucial in determining whether we shall succeed or not. Take for example the situation that a personnel manager is in: he usually has limited executive authority to wield when cajoling line management into behaving responsibly with the human resources at the organization's disposal. More often, he has to fall back on his skills of persuasion. As every wise personnel manager knows, it is not solely the *quality* of the suggestions he puts forward, in terms of their logic, practicability and so on that wins the day: certainly his personal credibility with the line is equally important. If the line management's observations of his previous behaviour has led it to have a low regard for him and the contribution he can make, even if he then comes up with a first class idea it is unlikely to be heeded.

Some people think that when personal credibility plays such a significant part in someone's success it is some sort of outrage and a rather cynical example of how gullible human beings are. Perhaps you believe that this emphasis on behaviour is rather trite and missing the point? Certainly some people are irritated to learn that the effort they put into arguing logically is often completely negated by their inability to arrange their accompanying behaviour appropriately.

This is not to suggest that our behaviour is the sole or even the most important factor in determining our effectiveness. But it is *one* of the factors and one that we can choose to harness to our advantage.

Let us take another example. The other day a salesman came to advise my wife on an efficient layout for her kitchen. He did not explicitly announce his objective but let us suppose that it was to win an order that would result in the firm he represented installing its kitchen furniture and fittings. He went about this task in a way that led my wife to conclude it was all rather a bore; just routine, done hundreds like it before. He asked relatively few questions. He grumbled a bit about some of the odd shapes in the kitchen explaining what a problem they were if all the space were to be fully used. He showed her pamphlets and sample working surfaces in rather a diffident take it or leave it way. He left promising to submit drawings and a full quotation for the work. The next day a salesman representing a competitive company came for his appointment. He was late as it happened but had telephoned to say so and to apologize in advance. As soon as he saw the kitchen he made complimentary comments. He didn't overdo it but left my wife with the impression that the kitchen with its odd shapes and angles had caught his interest. He asked my wife lots of questions about her needs and paid careful attention to her ideas. He actively supported many of them, developed others and suggested some alternatives, explaining their advantages. He had a squared sheet of paper in his brief case that he used to draw a plan of the kitchen and then placed model kitchen cabinets, sink units and so on in different positions to test my wife's reactions to alternative layouts. He left promising to submit drawings and a full quotation for the work.

When the quotations came they were remarkably similar. The cabinets they were proposing also looked much the same. The first salesman's use of one of the awkward corners was rather better than the other's. Despite this there was no doubt that the second salesman had won the order. His behaviour had been the deciding factor.

I know a managing director of a company who is enormously demanding in his behaviour. He has a reputation for being a stickler over detail. He asks devastatingly perceptive questions and has an uncanny knack of uncovering weaknesses and areas where people's knowledge is shaky and uncertain. He always plays devil's advocate; he rarely accepts presentations, ideas and proposals first time round and sends people scurrying back to dig out additional details. To cap it all, everything must always be done at once if not sooner. The effect that this behaviour has on his direct subordinates, all senior directors, is predictable. They have learned to keep their heads down and have developed various strategies to protect themselves. They are naturally reluctant to take decisions, they delay and procrastinate, they cause things to be worked and reworked to excess. They are forced to pay pathological attention to detail and to work overlong hours.

This manager's behaviour is of prime importance in affecting the working atmosphere and performance of his colleagues and ultimately, via them, of the whole organization. It may be that this managing director has thought about the consequences of behaving as he does. He may have decided that it is appropriate after taking stock of his directors and the state of the company. Be that as it may my concern at the moment is to show, through examples, that behaviour does make a significant difference to the behaviour of others and therefore, in turn to the results we achieve in face to face interaction.

I know a doctor in general practice who is the senior partner in a firm of doctors. He is short of patients. He has plenty on his register but they avoid actually seeing him because he treats his patients as if they are stupid. When they ring for an appointment at the surgery they ask for the junior partner. Yet the junior partner actually knows less, professionally, than the senior doctor. It is the difference in behaviour that accounts for the unpopularity of one and the high demand for the other. The same happens with clergy. Some have full churches, some have empty. The explanation is not always but usually to be found in the singer not the song.

Quite clearly behaviour is not the only factor that determines the success of salesmen, managers, doctors and clergy. A host of non-interactive skills play a part too: factors such as how hard they work, their technical or professional know-how, their temperament when it comes to making decisions, their basic stance towards people, whether for example they move away or towards other people. These and many more are all aspects of behaviour that distinguish between people. They are also examples of behaviour that does not necessarily play a large part in determining someone's *interactive* skills: the behaviour he uses when he is in face to face interaction with other people.

Other factors are involved in determining someone's success. These are those that are *external* to the actual person under consideration. Our managing director's success, for example, does not just hinge on his behavioural characteristics — interactive and non-interactive but also on factors like the size and performance of the company, the nature of its product, the competence of key people in the organization, the state of the market, competitors' activities and the financial climate.

Here is one further example to show behaviour in its proper perspective. The effectiveness of a personnel manager hinges not only on his interactive competence and personal credibility but also on other factors such as the enlightenment of members of line management as the consumers of personnel services, because they are so influential in shaping what those services shall be; the phase of development of the company, because there are differing pressures depending on whether it is in the 'establishing itself/entrepreneurial phase' or the 'consolidating/bedding down phase' or the 'slimming for survival phase'. Other examples include the funding of the personnel function, the trade unions because their activities make a vast difference to what the personnel manager can spend his time on and, not least, factors to do with the professional personnel expertise of the personnel manager and his subordinates and colleagues in the personnel function.

In summary, I hope to have shown at the outset that our behaviour in face to face interaction with other people is one among several factors that helps to determine our success and effectiveness. Behaviour, however, is a factor that many people choose to ignore or to acknowledge grudgingly. In part this is because they have not understood how it is possible deliberately to arrange and control their behaviour according to the circumstances in which they find themselves. There are also strong reservations about doing this. It is argued that to lay on a deliberate display of overt behaviour that is not necessarily an accurate reflection of the underlying feelings and attitudes is in some sense dishonest. But having straight, open dealings with people does not necessarily mean that you *have* to reveal your underlying feelings in your overt behaviour. Whether you do so or not depends on your analysis of the situation and the objectives you wish to achieve with the people with whom you are interacting.

There is another practical snag in allowing feelings to dictate behaviour. If, for example, you are feeling displeased with your secretary because she has misplaced something, the feelings may spill over into your behaviour in various ways. You could be rather brusque with her. You could criticize her work. You could suddenly return some of her typing when normally you accept it at that standard. You could actually say something like 'I must admit I'm feeling a bit cross with you today because you lost that letter that I needed for yesterday's meeting'. These are just four alternative ways in which your underlying feelings of annoyance might be reflected in your behaviour. The first three are ambiguous. They leave the secretary largely in the dark about why you are being brusque, hyper-critical and returning her work when normally you would accept it. She cannot possibly *know* why because, remember, she only has access to your behaviour and has to work backwards from what is observable to reach conclusions about underlying factors. This is how misunderstandings between people arise.

So even if you *are* going to allow your feelings to spill over into your overt behaviour you still, in many circumstances, need consciously to arrange the behaviour so that it achieves whatever you wish it to achieve without all sorts of unwanted consequences. Clearly there are many situations where it would be inappropriate to allow your underlying feelings to dictate your behaviour. In a delicate negotiation with the unions it can be cataclysmic to allow, say, feelings of frustration to burst out onto the behavioural surface. One of the joys of being interactively skilful is that you can deliberately engineer your overt behaviour to give the desired impression and not be at the mercy of your subjective feelings. There is a time and a place for subjective feelings, a time and a place for you to blow your top, and even a time and a place for relaxing behaviourally and not giving it conscious thought.

Just when is it worth going to the trouble consciously to arrange and control behaviour? The short answer to that is this: whenever you are in a situation where you are conscious of wanting to achieve something, of having some objectives in fact, then it behoves you to arrange your overt behaviour so that it facilitates the achievement of those objectives. Objectives, rather than feelings, dictate behaviour. Whenever you have objectives to persuade or influence people or to impress them, your behaviour is a critical factor in determining the outcome. When you are in prickly situations, where emotions are running high and one ill-considered word can be a turning point, your behaviour is crucial. Whenever you are in a situation where the people present have conflicting objectives, behaviour is crucial in steering the interaction through to a fruitful conclusion.

On the other hand, on many interactive occasions we are not actively conscious of wishing to achieve an objective: when we relax at the bar with friends for example, when we pass the time of day in inconsequential chit chat with people. I hesitate to say 'at home' with our families because perhaps one of the reasons why there is often so much strife on the home front is because people reckon it is safe to 'relax'; consequently, behaviour is often abominable in all sorts of crucial family interactions when objectives go unheeded and behaviour is not arranged accordingly. Few would seriously doubt that the way parents behave in their dealings with their children is enormously influential in their development, and the same applies to teachers. A fascinating experiment in America demonstrated just how powerful a factor the behaviour of teachers is. Having tested the intelligence of vast numbers of children in different schools and towns, the experimenters leaked news back to certain teachers about the performance of certain children. Unbeknown to the teachers the news was false. They would let it slip that so and so was a lad with a lot of potential when he had in fact put in a below average performance on the intelligence tests. The teachers were of course very surprised about this, so much so that they modified their behaviour towards the pupils in question — small things like giving them more time, being more encouraging and showing less exasperation. One year later the whole experiment was repeated. Hundreds of children were rated for intelligence and the pupils where false news had been leaked back had all made bigger improvements, measured in an increase in IQ points than was average for the sample. There were other variables at work but clearly the teachers' behaviour was the big factor in determining this change: another instance of the crucial influence of overt behaviour.

SUMMARY

We defined interactive skills as those used in face to face encounters when arranging behaviour so that it is in step with objectives. Behaviour was also defined as everything we do, verbal and non-verbal, which is overt and therefore directly observable by others.

This definition was used to distinguish between behaviour

itself and underlying factors such as attitudes, motives and feelings. We found that behaviour is visible and thus makes a more direct impact on the behaviour of others. Attitudes are invisible and can only show themselves in behaviour itself.

We moved on to explore the relationship between personality and behaviour. Personality was found to be an all embracing term setting overall limits on what we could do. The constraints imposed by our personalities, however, left plenty of room for behavioural adaptation.

One of the main objects of this chapter was to give examples to show that behaviour is a factor that can make a considerable difference to our interactive performance. We saw how behaviour is one factor among others that conspire together to determine our success or failure.

Finally, we argued that more attention would be paid to behaviour as an influential factor if more people knew how to set about arranging and controlling it. We finished by identifying when it is worth troubling consciously to arrange behaviour. The short answer was that it was worth doing so whenever we were in a face to face situation and consciously aware of wishing to achieve some objective.

2 Situations, objectives and behaviour

The remainder of this book has to be based on certain assumptions. This is because the behavioural area is relatively fraught with uncertainty and half truths. Opinions on many major issues still outweigh hard black and white facts in the behavioural sciences. This is why it is only fair to share explicitly the assumptions that underpin this book. I am admitting to some of my biases and prejudices at the outset so that you can compare them with yours and have early warning of any mismatch.

The first assumption is that the way we behave in face to face encounters with people *does* matter; that our behaviour affects the behaviour of others and therefore in turn, the results we achieve. This assumption was explored in the last chapter to the extent that I hope you can join me in subscribing to it, at any rate, for the time being.

The second main assumption is that there is no single panacea-like correct behaviour style. This is an inconvenient thing to believe. It would obviously simplify things greatly to have a well-proven behavioural approach that stands us in good stead in all situations, with all people, always. Unfortunately, behavioural rights and wrongs are more difficult to come by. Our experience should tell us that if the situations and the people we encounter vary, our behavioural approach should vary also. Sometimes the variations in approach need only be slight. Sometimes they will need to be considerable. The point is that the rights and wrongs of behaviour only make sense in the light of situations, other people and objectives. There is no panacea. This explains why, maddeningly, behavioural scientists always hedge their answers with expressions like 'it all depends'. One manager was recently relieved to learn that the appropriateness or inappropriateness of his behaviour depended on the circumstances of the situation he was dealing with at the time. 'At least', he said, 'that means that by sheer chance I'm bound to be right *some of the time!*' In a sense he was right. There *is* a time and a place for most behaviours.

Thirdly, and this chapter is mainly concerned with developing this assumption, I am assuming that the maxim 'If you have got objectives, your behaviour should be in step with them' is not too sweeping a Great Truth. It will show how objectives can provide a meaningful backcloth against which to view behaviour and there will be some examples to demonstrate the usefulness of this in-step-out-of-step concept. This is a relatively easy way of making judgements about the appropriateness of your own as well as other people's behaviour.

The fourth assumption is the most contentious. It is that on many occasions we need *consciously* to organize our behaviour. In fact, this assumption tends to follow from the first three. If you subscribe to them, inevitably you must conclude that behaviour needs to be consciously 'arranged' to fit the bill on many occasions. Let us just check that: in summary the first three assumptions were that behaviour *does* matter; that there is no single correct behaviour style; and that behaviour should be 'in step' with objectives. Is the need to plan, organize and control behaviour an inevitable consequence of these?

There are, certainly staunch objectors to this last assumption. Many people treasure the spontaneity of behaviour above all else, arguing that it is 'dishonest' deliberately to lay on a display of overt behaviour that, for example, does not reflect underlying feelings accurately enough. Does this mean that we should allow our feelings to dictate our behaviour? If so, all sorts of standards of behaviour that have been built into our society are going to have to change. It means we could 'blow our tops' just when we felt like it irrespective of the consequences, we could break down and cry just when we felt like it, we could go silent and not speak to people just when we felt like it. Surely a much sounder basis is to let our objectives dictate our behaviour? To do so helps us to understand that on some occasions it is entirely appropriate to allow our feelings to spill out into our overt behaviour and that on others it is not. The objectives become the key, not feelings.

This leads one to conclude that it is rather more dishonest to conceal our *objectives* from people than it is to conceal our feelings. As I shall show later, one of the hallmarks of an interactively skilled person is that they frequently declare their objectives openly and explicitly. Even if they do not declare them, it should be easy for others to *work them out*. If the behaviour is 'in step' then the objectives will, to some extent, be transparent.

Another objection that people make to the notion that behaviour should be organized and controlled is that to do so sets up internal stresses that are bad for you. They argue that the effort involved in consciously controlling behaviour, instead of relaxing and letting it 'rip', takes its toll over time and gives people breakdowns, ulcers, coronaries and the like! But an enlightened person who has mastered the skills involved in consciously arranging behaviour can do this without stress. *Learning* the skills is stressful but this applies to the acquisition of any skill. When you are learning to ride a bicycle, drive a car or speak in public, this is also stressful. Once the skills have been acquired the stress abates and the conscious effort required to perform skilfully is perfectly manageable.

The internal stresses argument can take another form. The argument goes like this: if I am having constantly to hide my 'true' feelings and lay on a 'contrived' display of overt behaviour when I am interacting with people, day in day out, this will cause such a build up of internal tensions that sooner or later something will have to give. Notice that this argument tends to assume that stress results from the effort required to arrange behaviour so that it does not reflect underlying feelings and emotions. It is certainly true that when there is a poor match between feelings and behaviour the effort required to bottle up the feelings is wearing. But an interactively skilled person is not likely to be in this situation as often as an unskilled one. For a start the skilled person, by definition, finds it easier, and therefore *less* stressful, to control behaviour. Secondly, the skilled person is much clearer about *when* to control behaviour and when not to. In other words internal stresses are *reduced* as you become more skilful. Furthermore, the skilful, insightful practitioner of interactive skills understands that his interactions with people *are* frequently going to be stressful and plans 'safe' ways of releasing the stresses. A quota of sports and pastimes, planned relaxation, some form of meditation perhaps, all these and many others can be used to work off the stresses and ensure that behaviour in face to face encounters is nicely controlled and compatible with whatever the objectives of the occasion are.

One final point on stress: a main source of cumulative stress is failure itself — the constant bruising effect of failing to achieve your objectives, the nagging suspicion that you could have handled that better; the unpleasant ambiguity of not being able to put your finger on what went wrong — or even *if* something *did* go wrong. These are the stuff of which stress is made. An interactively skilled person has a better 'hit rate' in terms of achieving objectives in interaction than an unskilled person. The better the hit rate the less the stress. An interactively skilled person even considers failure to be an opportunity to learn and this quest to learn from mistakes and actively strive for improvement cushions the bruising still further.

Another frequent objection to the suggestion that behaviour be consciously organized and controlled is that to do so would not be fair to other people. How would the people on the receiving end of our behaviour know the 'real' us? Would they be confused if we behaved differently on different occasions? Would they suspect that we were non-genuine or inconsistent? Worse still, would they condemn us as guilty of manipulation and Machiavellian practices? Two points need to be made here. First, the bit of us that is real to other people *is* our behaviour because, as we have already established, it is visible. So, however we behave, it is real to other people. Secondly, worries about manipulation and inconsistency tend to abate when you realize that interactive skills tend to push for increased openness and explicitness in relationships with people. This is the reverse of the connotations that most people have in connection with manipulation. Manipulation is considered by most people to be a furtive, clandestine way of influencing people. Innocent victims are engineered into something and — this is an important ingredient of manipulation also — realize *afterwards* what happened: too late to avert it but early enough to resent it.

Such goings-on are nothing whatever to do with the proper use of interactive skills. Interactive skills are not about being furtive, they are about being transparent. They are not about confusing people and keeping them in the dark, they are about behaving clearly and in so doing getting clear behaviours in return. They are not about hidden motives and facades but about explicit objectives and authentic, in step behaviours.

Let us explore one final objection before going on to spend the remainder of this chapter establishing the links between situations, objectives and behaviour.

An objection often levelled is: how can we be expected to organize and plan our behaviour? We have not time! We spend too much time planning already and all to no avail; more often than not we have to ditch the plan because it turns out to be unrealistic anyway.

The theoretical answer to this is that planning actually saves time in the end. Instead of unproductive, rambling meetings, planning helps to cut the overall time and push up productivity. But the problem with this sort of answer is that people react by claiming that they have not even the time to invest in the initial planning necessary to reap the eventual reward of time savings. It is rather like giving someone with no capital advice about how they could invest their money profitably if only they had some. A more realistic way of overcoming the objection is to show that planning is *not* synonymous with preparing. Planning can only be done beforehand if we have time to do it and if we have sufficient advance information on which to base the plan. When it comes to the business of interacting with other people these two prerequisites are often not met. Countless interactions spring up spontaneously and many can develop into interactions of a crucial nature. It is commonplace to hear that all the vital decisions are taken in the dining room over lunch, or during casual encounters in corridors or even in lavatories! Frequently, then, we are unprepared in the sense that we have not had a chance to plan beforehand.

Beforehand planning is not the only sort of planning there is. It is quite possible to plan in a much more on-going, dynamic sense and this is far more important in the rough and tumble of face to face interactions than static, preparatory planning activities. On-going planning requires us to size up the situation *as we are in it*, with the interaction already developing. It requires us actively to think about what we want to achieve within the life of the interaction and how best to arrange our visible behaviour so that we are successful. This sort of planning does not call for any extra time. It merely requires a more disciplined conscious approach during interactions. It also requires us to be equally alert to behavioural issues and content issues in parallel, a skill that we shall pinpoint more carefully in a later chapter.

This emphasis on on-going planning does not exclude the possibility of beforehand planning. You may have many interactions where you know about them in advance and have sufficient information to do some preparatory planning. You may frequently instigate interactions yourself, for example, rather than participating in discussions initiated by other people. You may have advance notice of key interactions where you judge that it is crucial to plan your approach beforehand. Typical examples might include a salesman calling on a likely prospect, a personnel manager preparing for a tricky negotiation, a job candidate going to a selection interview, a manager preparing to appraise one of his subordinates.

The remainder of this book proceeds on the assumption that you believe your behaviour to be an important enough factor in your people dealings to want to get better at consciously organizing and controlling it.

THE LINKS BETWEEN SITUATIONS, OBJECTIVES AND BEHAVIOUR

The concept to be introduced in this section falls into the 'You know it makes sense' category. Conceptually people have little trouble in both absorbing it and subscribing to it. Furthermore, the concept is not new. The snag, in common with most 'You know it makes sense' concepts, is in actually doing it. It is patently obvious that there is often such a wide gulf between *knowing* something and doing it that many people fail to bridge it. Frequently heavy smokers, for example, will accept that smoking is damaging to health but continue to do it. Compulsive eaters will accept that their eating habits cause weight problems but continue to eat between meals. The difference between knowing and doing is evident in many aspects of human behaviour: motorway 'madness', not wearing seat belts, not using time fruitfully enough, not saving energy, not observing proven safety precautions — the list is endless. Knowing is clearly not in itself a sufficient prerequisite for doing.

The warning then is that the concept that follows requires practical skill to translate it beyond mere knowledge into action. That said, let us look at the concept itself.

We have already had to qualify much of the discussion on behaviour by pointing out that what is appropriate behaviourally depends intimately on other factors. The simple truth is that behaviour does not make sense unless it is viewed within the confines of a specific set of circumstances. It follows that behaviour is, at best, a *means* and that for the *ends* we need to look beyond behaviour itself.

The total framework is, first, to be in touch with the reality of the 'people' situations we encounter; secondly, to be clear about what objectives it is realistic to attempt to achieve; and thirdly, to be able to arrange behaviour so that it is in step with those objectives. Rather than develop this in the abstract, here is an example to show how it is possible to use this framework to link the circumstances of a situation, objectives and behaviour together in a tight bond.

The situation first: suppose that you have just taken over as manager from a colleague who considered that he was not doing his job properly unless he *told* his subordinates what to do and scrutinized closely to check that they did it. Your first impressions are that your predecessor's behaviour style had had the effect of stifling ideas amongst your new team. This is a disappointment to you because you want them to be aware that you not only welcome but expect ideas and suggestions from them. You decide to set about opening up communications between you and them so that they can become less wary of committing themselves and more forward in producing ideas. Furthermore, you decide to get this process started by inviting your direct reports to a meeting.

Obviously in real life you would know much more than the bare bones this description of the situation offers. You would, for example, know all sorts of extra points about the way the subordinates had behaved so far in interaction with you as their new boss. You would know some of the individual differences that were characteristic of them.

The next step is to allow the circumstances of this situation to contaminate your decisions about what objective you will strive to achieve in the meeting. Opinions on how far you can go in one initial get together with your direct reports will vary, depending on all sorts of differences in emphasis and perception that we make in our reading of the situation just described. Some will feel it best to soft pedal and just have a relaxing 'getting to know each other better' type of meeting. Others will judge that to be an unambitious flavour for the meeting and want to pitch in immediately with more specific objectives and a more tangible output. More will be said about the process of judging what it is realistic to achieve in the next chapter, where we focus attention on objectives.

Here is an example of the sort of objective you might decide to aim for in the circumstances of the situation just described.

To run the meeting in such a way that my subordinates have been encouraged to come up with lots of ideas and suggestions.
I shall have achieved this success fully if:

- each subordinate present has produced at least three suggestions by the end of the meeting
- we have agreed that at least half the suggestions are worthy of further exploration/action
- the meeting finishes within one and a half hours of its starting time
- at least a third of the participants spontaneously remark that the meeting has been useful/rewarding/involving and the like.

Notice that this objective is couched in fairly specific terms and pinpoints the state of affairs that we wish to exist by the time the meeting ends. The merits of this sort of construction, or housestyle, will be discussed in chapter four. Meanwhile your attention should be drawn to the immediacy of the objective. It relates to the interaction itself and only has a one and a half hour life. This is a vital characteristic because we want the objective to guide us in deciding how to behave during this particular face to face interaction. If the objective was more far reaching or more general, it is unlikely that it would circumscribe behaviour adequately.

The final step in the process is to think about how best to behave in order to maximize the probability of achieving the objective. Here is an example of a behaviour approach that is in step with the objective.

Since they are unlikely to be able to respond spontaneously to any pleas from me for suggestions, I'll give them plenty of advance warning about the meeting. I will deliberately choose a topic for the meeting where the likelihood that they will have lots of reasonable ideas is high. I'll circulate news of the topic together with the suggestion that they think about it beforehand and come to the meeting with some ideas at the ready. At the meeting I'll start it off by asking them if they have any ideas on 'measures' that we could apply to our current meeting to judge its success together at the conclusion. If they haven't any ideas on this then I'll put one up, tentatively, as an Aunt Sally, hoping to spark off some further suggestions from them. I'll adopt a similar strategy over the plan for how the meeting should proceed; asking them for suggestions first and, only if that fails, putting some forward myself. Whenever they put forward a suggestion, I'll react to it in a positive way by supporting it or seeking clarification to get some aspect clearer. I will not disagree with any suggestions during this particular meeting nor will I play devil's advocate, however tempting that reaction might be. I'll write all their suggestions down and read them back to check that I have understood/recorded them correctly. At the conclusion of the meeting I will invite them to join me in applying the success measures which we agreed at the outset and, in particular, to check on whether at least half the recorded suggestions are worthy of further exploration/action.

Every bit of this plan is heavily contaminated by the objective. The behavioural stance will need to be mainly seeking and supportive. Telling behaviours and other sorts of reactions are to be curbed lest they jeopardize the accomplishment of the objective. It will therefore be necessary throughout the meeting consciously to control behaviour so that it remains in step with the objective.

The problems of keeping behaviour in step with objectives are very real. I know that I frequently catch my behaviour drifting beyond the parameters set by the objective I am aiming for. This is not too difficult to spot in others too, providing you have some inkling of their objective. Here are some examples observed recently.

The personnel director who met me in order to assess my capabilities in relation to an assignment he was setting up. He actually started our meeting by saying, quite explicitly, that he wanted to spend an hour or so learning about my experience/expertise and not spending much time describing the problem/assignment as he saw it on this occasion. Two hours later I was still trying to get a word in edgeways!

The salesman who solemnly told me that whenever he was faced with a prospect who was a 'low reactor' (someone who neither agrees nor disagrees but just plays it deadpan) his tactic was to step up his rate of open-ended questioning and to tolerate relatively long pauses thus 'forcing' the client to react. When I accompanied him on some sales calls I found he did the exact opposite! He stepped *up* his sales patter, dropped his questioning rate and filled every silence by talking nineteen to the dozen.

The manager who started a problem solving meeting by saying how important it was to talk all round the problem and to respect everyone's different points of view, etc. and then proceeded to bamboozle everyone into his way of thinking, shooting down alternative views of the problem and effectively gagging everyone present.

The personnel manager who told me how important it was for him to gain personal credibility with the line managers with whom he was about to have a session and went on to blind and bore them with personnel jargon.

Examples of the difficulty of keeping behaviour in step with objectives extend beyond face to face encounters. Politicians are often suspect on this count. People are frequently at a loss to square political actions with the declared objectives. When President Ford pardoned ex-President Nixon, for example, there was an uproar because people saw this as a piece of behaviour that was out of step with the objective declared by President Ford: that it was his priority to restore confidence in the White House administration by being seen to be straight and honest in all their dealings. These sorts of out of stepness lead to credibility gaps, an erosion of trust, and to sinister reputations based on assumptions of deceit and double-dealing. If the observed behaviour is out of step with the declared objectives then only two conclusions are possible. The most charitable is that the person is unable to control his behaviour so that it is in step with his objectives. The other is that the person has hidden objectives that differ from the ones he declared and that the private objectives are more instrumental in shaping his behaviour than the public ones.

BEHAVIOUR AND OBJECTIVES: IN STEP AND OUT OF STEP RELATIONSHIPS

Let us explore this concept of objectives and behaviour by using a blow by blow transcript of an interaction. In the excerpt that follows David is personnel director. Two of his subordinates are present. Chris has been in personnel for many years but has only recently been appointed manager of a new unit called the Organization Development Centre (ODC). Fred is the personnel director's administrative assistant.

As you will see, they are meeting a little in advance of a scheduled meeting between them and George, the company's director of training, and Ian who is manager of the management training unit (MTU).

As you read through the transcript of the conversation try to decide which contributions are in step and which out of step with the following objectives:

David's objective:

To have agreed what they want to achieve in the meeting with George and Ian.
David would have been successful if:

- They had agreed that the objective was to sort out the boundaries between the ODC and MTU
- He had secured Chris's agreement to postpone any ideas of amalgamating the ODC and MTU.

Chris's objective:

To have got David's agreement to allocate both extra accommodation and extra help for the ODC.
Chris would have been successful if:

- David had sanctioned Chris's request for a conference room
- David had named one of his other direct reports as the person to help out on one of the projects.

With these objectives in mind, here is a verbatim account of what was said.

1 David   Right, Chris, we've got just 15 minutes or so to talk about this afternoon's meeting before George and Ian get here. Where do you want to come out of it?

2 Chris   Just before we do that, I wanted to have a word about accommodation for the OD centre. You remember I sent you a note on it. . . .

3 David   Look! I'm under enough pressure to cut down on the ODC in its initial stages as it is without you asking for a whole suite of conference rooms.

4 Chris   I'm not asking for a suite of rooms, only for one biggish conference room where senior clients can meet in an atmosphere conducive to problem solving.

5 David   Well, I'm warning you that the ODC image is a luxury I can't afford just now. Personnel's budget is under fire. We're likely to have to absorb a 10 per cent cut at any minute.

6 Chris   Well, you know my views on that. If the MD squeezes the personnel function any harder there won't be a worthwhile service left. He's cutting off his nose to spite his face.

7 David   Okay, okay. Let's talk about that another time. Now, what about this afternoon's meeting? Right now I don't feel clear enough about what we want to get out of it.

8	Chris	So I can't change your mind about accommodation for the ODC?
9	David	I thought I'd made it clear. If you are responsible for setting up a project you are also responsible for housing it. Fight it out with the others along that corridor. If you can persuade them they need less space then you can have your conference room.
10	Chris	But that's not fair! I have never gained the impression that I was supposed to *fight* for office accommodation that the ODC *must* have if it is to function properly. Once you had backed the centre, agreed its budget and so on I naturally assumed that other necessary facilities would be forthcoming.
11	David	I consider this whole issue to be a very small point within the total compass of what has to be achieved. You don't need to bring these small problems to me.
12	Chris	Well, I'm sorry but I don't see it as a small problem. If the centre isn't housed adequately then it can't function properly and that's all there is to it.
13	Fred	If you want me to come and act as a referee between you and the others I'll gladly do so, but I'm inclined to agree that it's a relatively small point.
14	David	Good. Now let's move on.
15	Chris	I just hope you've registered my disapproval over the handling of this whole thing. When I took on this job I naturally assumed that I would have sufficient support to make it viable. . . .
16	David	In this climate you can't afford to assume anything. I don't and so I can't see why you should be able to. I continue to hold you totally responsible for the establishment of a successful organization development centre.
17	Chris	While we're on the subject that brings me to another point. The sales engineering project

has got to the point where it needs an extra pair of hands. I can't chair all the workshops myself. It means that other projects aren't getting enough attention.

18 David Why don't you get the two personnel managers involved? Tim Brown in sales and Stephen Jones in engineering? You can't do it *for* them. All we can expect the centre to do is *start* projects of that kind. But once they are launched they should be handed over to the local personnel people.

19 Chris Yes, but both Tim and Stephen are already complaining of being over-committed without this. They are too busy fire fighting on the industrial relations front to have time left to resource a project like this.

20 David Then perhaps that tells us something.

21 Chris Like what? That the personnel managers are busy doing the wrong things?

22 David No. That if personnel managers are busy with the short term you have got a problem in winning some of their time for a longer term project like the sales engineering one.

23 Chris Well, with respect, we all know that already. Surely the trick is to see how short term needs can be dealt with to long term advantage?

24 Fred Or to take long term issues and make them attractive in the short term?

25 David It has to be that way or else we shall be accused of not working for the good of the business; just for our own professional self-interest. We are under enough pressure as it is.

26 Chris Well, I'm telling you that *I'm* under pressure to find someone to chair those meetings! I don't think I'll succeed in getting either Tim or Stephen to take it on somehow.

27 David Look! I'm definitely going to have to make choices about the deployment of resources in personnel HQ. If the personnel managers in the divisions are asking for extra help on indus-

trial relations and compensation issues . . .
well, let's put it this way . . . we must put the
resources where the pressure is.

28   Chris   I think you've changed your views on the role
of personnel HQ and the divisions.

29   David   Well, it's clear that we haven't yet convinced
the divisional personnel managers about the
need for the OD centre. I've always been clear
that HQ has a dual role: to provide support to
the divisions *and* to look ahead and have some
forward plans. As far as I'm concerned we need
an OD centre but we are going to have it with
the blessing of the divisional personnel
managers. That's your priority. If it takes
another year just getting their support it will
be worth it.

30   David's   Excuse me, sorry to interrupt but George is
      Sec.   here. Are you ready for him?

31   David   Just hang on to him for a minute or two will
you, Sue? Now come on, Chris, we haven't
planned this meeting at all. What do you want
to achieve?

32   Chris   I thought it was your meeting. You called it
after all. What objectives did you have in
mind?

33   David   I thought we needed it to clear up the boundaries between your centre and George's
management training team. Weren't you
complaining of overlaps and fuzzy terms of
reference?

34   Chris   Well, I don't know if I'd put it as strongly as
complaining — but I do think it would help to
try and straighten out who is supposed to do
what — yes.

35   David   So how do you want to play it? I'd be inclined
to sit George next to me and let him tell us
all about it. I agree that we've got to get the
responsibilities of the centre and management
training sorted out. Just because the centre has
got off to rather a shaky start that's no reason

to have management training tarred with the same brush. I feel duty bound to point this out to George. We're ready for them now aren't we?

36   Fred   I wouldn't have thought so but we can't keep them waiting any longer. Shall I fetch them in?

37   Chris   Just a minute. I've got a feeling that we aren't agreed at all. Listening to what you've just said, David . . . it leaves me wondering why we are having this meeting at all. Are we going to suggest that the centre and management training amalgamate or not? I thought that was the original idea.

38   David   Lord no! I'm saying that we can't do that now because of the poor reputation of the centre. If it had got off to a better start, that would have been a different matter . . . quite a different matter. I now think its a better idea to leave them separated organizationally but to work out the overlaps and so on. Get them in please, Fred.

How did David and Chris fare in your estimation? Do you agree that neither was very successful in achieving his objectives? David failed to get the objectives for the meeting with George and Ian agreed and he was certainly nowhere near to securing Chris's agreement to no amalgamation, as we see from Chris's outburst in 37. With quite different objectives, Chris hasn't done too well either. He came away without a conference room and without one of David's direct reports assigned to the sales engineering project.

What went wrong? Probably at least three things.

First, the two men had quite different objectives. This meant that in a short time like 15 minutes there was a struggle over whose objectives should dominate. Different though they were, given a longer interaction both sets of objectives could have been achieved. In the circumstances you might feel that one of the protagonists should have backed off in the interests of *some* progress. I agree, and feel it should have been Chris since it became clear very quickly that the accomplishment of his objectives was unlikely in the circumstances. In fact, the more he strove to achieve them the more certain was his failure. This means that his failure was, in part, due to having a poor judgement about the objectives it was feasible to go for within the circumstances of the situation.

Secondly, too many of David's behaviours were out of step with his objective. He started out in step (1) and he finished more or less in step (31, 33, 35 and 37) but he allowed the influence of Chris's behaviour to push him into an out of step position for most of the time (3, 5, 9, 11, 16, 18, 20, 22, 25, 27 and 29). He tried to get back in step a couple of times (7 and 14) but Chris always managed to drag him off course again. My final balance sheet for David shows that out of 18 behaviours only 7 were in step. I conclude that he deserved to fail. It wasn't just Chris's fault.

Thirdly, far too many of Chris's behaviours were out of step with his objective. He, like David, also started out in step (2 and 4) but *starting* in step is relatively easy. It is *keeping* in step that is difficult. He slips out of step very quickly, falling an easy prey to some of his pet gripes and hobby horses (6, 21, 23 and 28 are the most flagrant examples). When you remember that Chris's objectives were all about securing David's agreement and cooperation in various ways it is easy to see that many of his reactions to David were badly out of step (10, 12, 15, 19 and 26). Over-all, in the passage up to 30 where David's secretary interrupts to say that George is waiting, Chris only has four of his 13 behaviours in step (2, 4, 8 and 17) and of these 4 and 8 are suspect if we take other behavioural nuances into account.

Both men did badly if we merely view their behaviour against their own personal objectives. By the time we view their behaviour in interaction, with different objectives pulling them in different directions, the result is an unsatisfactory failure for both. Both men are responsible. Either of them could have used more in step behaviours to have salvaged the situation.

In the next chapter there are two more transcripts to give

you practice in using objectives as a backcloth for identifying in step and out of step behaviours.

One of the transcripts traces David through the meeting with George and Ian. The other introduces new characters and is based on an appraisal discussion situation.

SUMMARY

The chapter opened by declaring four basic assumptions that underpin the interactive skills approach: that behaviour in face to face encounters does affect the outcome; that behaviour needs to vary from situation to situation; that behaviour should be in step with objectives; that behaviour frequently needs to be consciously organized and controlled.

Some of the common objections to these assumptions — particularly the last — were explored. Issues touched on were the honesty/dishonesty of having underlying feelings that were not expressed in overt behaviour; the problem of internal stress arising from the effort needed consciously to maintain a particular display of overt behaviour; the problem of manipulation and inconsistency in our dealings with people. Finally, the problems of finding time to plan and organize behaviour.

The remainder of the chapter was spent showing how situations, objectives and behaviour itself act as a complex system where alterations in any one inevitably has repercussions for the others. In particular, the idea that there should be a vital bond between objectives and behaviour was explored. A number of illustrations were used to show how judgements about the appropriateness of behaviour can be made in the light of objectives.

3 Exercises in Behaviour Recognition

This chapter is devoted to two case studies in the form of transcripts. The idea is to give you further practice in relating behaviour to objectives before moving on to look at both objectives and behaviour in more detail in subsequent chapters.

Of course there are limitations to this sort of case study approach. Unlike real life, transcripts are in writing and this both helps and hinders the analytical process. It *helps* by having everything captured in writing so that we look back at what was said as many times as we wish. It *hinders* because the verbatim account only tells us what was said and starves us of other accompanying behavioural information that we have access to in real life. Intonation, for example, facial expressions and the whole gamut of non-verbal behaviours are largely left to the imagination.

The other major limitation is that these case studies are exclusively about *other people* and not about ourselves. The skill of spotting in step and out of step behaviour in others is not an adequate replacement for the skill needed to monitor and control our own behavioural performance. This you can only practise in your real-life interactions. Later chapters will show you how to work out objectives, how to plan behaviour and how to monitor behaviour. For the time being the practical rule of thumb, or technique, is consciously and continually to ask yourself two questions: 'What do I want to achieve in this interaction?' and, 'Is my behaviour in step with it'? If your answer to the first is 'I don't know', 'I'm not sure' or 'I don't want to achieve anything really', then you need not bother with the second question at all. If you are not consciously aware of wishing to achieve an objective then you can afford to freewheel behaviourally. This is because you can neither be in nor out of step with no objectives. One word of warning: if you find that for, say, a quarter of your interactive time you have no objectives and are accordingly behaviourally listless, you are in trouble. Such a high level of purposeless activity should be queried and I shall take this up in the next chapter along with some other crucial issues connected directly with objectives and indirectly with behaviour.

FIRST CASE STUDY

Let us follow the characters we introduced in the last chapter through the second part of their meeting. You will remember that David, the personnel director and Chris, manager of the newly established organization development centre, were preparing to interact with George, director of training and Ian, manager of the management training unit. Throughout the verbatim account that follows concentrate on analysing David's behaviour using the following objectives as your frame of reference:

David's objective: to have defined the responsibilities of the ODC and MTU in such a way that everyone is clear and cooperation between the two units is more likely.
  David will have been successful if:

- The main responsibilities of ODC and MTU have been listed and areas of potential overlap identified
- He has specifically said that he doesn't think it appropriate to merge ODC and MTU at present
- George and/or Ian have volunteered to work with him and/or Chris on at least one specific project or activity
- George and Ian leave the meeting making unsolicited

remarks about how useful it has been in clearing the air, tidying up grey areas and the like.

With this objective in mind analyse David's behaviour in the following transaction:

Enter George and Ian

1	David	Sorry to have kept you waiting, gentlemen.
2	George	That's all right. It's been quite useful really. Given Ian and myself time to collect our wits a bit.
3	David	Fine. Well would you like to start off? What can we do for you?
4	George	Best if Ian explains really I think. He's the chap who's done the homework.
5	Ian	Oh dear! What a build up. Well, as I understand it we are here to work out what to do to educate management throughout the company — overseas as well as here in the UK — so that they understand the MD's management style. A number of ideas have been bandied around ranging from the suggestion that the MD runs a series of seminars himself to the suggestion that someone studies his style closely enough to become an authority on it!
6	George	Yes, that puts it very fairly I think. The MD is certainly keen to find some economical way of getting his philosophy across. He seems pretty exasperated that people don't read him more easily.
7	David	In my view there is no substitute for an eyeball to eyeball encounter for this sort of thing. Best thing would be to have the MD sort this out with his direct reports and then have it cascade down in a series of workshops. As a matter of fact we did this in the personnel department when I took over. We had him here for a couple of

hours while we quizzed him. It worked very well didn't it Fred?

8 Fred   Yes, everyone thought it very valuable. We taped it all too so there is a transcript of the whole thing. Would that be an idea I wonder? How about getting the MD to do a video cassette? It means he only needs to do the session once and it could go out to all the overseas territories.

9 Ian   Would he be prepared to produce a video?

10 George Oh I would think so. If we put it to him the right way. I should think he'd be rather flattered.

11 David I've got my doubts. The MD doesn't spend time *talking* about a philosophy of management. He only ever talks about specific managerial problems. I just can't envisage anyone getting him to sustain a conversation on something as general as his management style — or anyone else's for that matter.

12 Ian   So what would you suggest then David?

13 David Perhaps we could feed him some questions aimed at getting his views on some specific problems. If we chose the questions carefully his answers could provide the clues we need on the more general aspects of his attitudes, style and what-have-you.

14 Chris In my experience telling him he has some problems isn't very successful. His attitude seems to be 'I don't have any problems. My subordinates have the problems'.

15 David I wasn't suggesting that we tell him he has problems. I was merely proposing that we draw up a list of questions that are carefully designed to reveal his management style without directly appearing to do so.

16 Chris I think he'd be smart enough to see through that.

17 George So what do *you* think would work, Chris?

		It sounds as if you don't favour the MD being involved at all?
18	Chris	No, I don't really. I think it would be best to have someone track the MD through a number of ordinary working days, observing his style until such time as he — the observer that is — can pinpoint the salient features of his approach and draw up a programme to explain it to others.
19	Ian	Who would be the best person to take on such a project?
20	David	Well, I personally think that someone from your management training unit would be best qualified for that sort of assignment, Ian.
21	George	Yes, Ian's people have clocked up a lot of experience on various tracking assignments.
22	Chris	Would it seem a little odd that this was a personnel project being carried out by someone from *outside* the personnel department?
23	Fred	Well I don't think anyone has designated this as a personnel project exactly. Would it matter whether it was headed up in personnel or in training? I can't think that it would. So long as the objective is achieved what does it matter?
24	David	I'd certainly like to propose that you take it on, Ian, in conjunction with Chris here. Surely this would be a good opportunity to cooperate?
25	Chris	Well I'm sorry. I quite definitely think this is one for the OD centre. When it was set up we made it quite clear that it would operate at director level in the company. I need hardly point out that the MD *is* a director level client! It will only cause confusion if an assignment of this kind goes to another unit.

26	David	I wasn't suggesting that Ian's people do it in isolation. I think it important that this is tackled as a joint project. You need to get together to work it out, to cooperate, decide who is going to do what and so on. I strongly urge that the actual tracking — if it comes to that — is done by Ian or one of his people. We need to tap their sort of expertise on a job like this.
27	Ian	How do you mean 'if it comes to that?' I was under the impression that we had agreed to tackle this as a tracking assignment.
28	David	Well at this stage I'd rather leave the options open. As far as I'm concerned I leave it to you and Chris to come up with proposals.
29	George	Hang on then! Does that mean we are any further forward? I thought *this* meeting was supposed to agree a course of action. What's the use of postponing it? We'll only need to meet a second time to consider the proposals.
30	David	I'm only suggesting that as a way forward because we don't seem to be agreed on any one definitive way of going about this. It also seems to me to be a golden opportunity to get these two working together for once instead of rowing about who does what. We all work for the same company after all.
31	Ian	Well, I'm happy to work closely with Chris on this but I feel it is important to clear up some of the ambiguity by appointing a project leader. Is that to be Chris or myself, or someone else?
32	David	Well, in view of the fact that the OD centre has more organizational prestige I would suggest Chris heads it up. This could be a

useful forerunner to actual amalgamation between the two units.

33	George	Sorry old boy. Who said anything about amalgamation? As I've told you before that'll happen over my dead body and not before. Anyway, we didn't come here to talk about that. Are we agreed on this MD thing then?
34	David	I'm surprised you come out so strongly against joining the two units together, George. I see it as a considerable advantage to both sides. It enhances the OD centre and provides them with manpower and skills they need. It also gets the management training unit reporting in at an appropriate level. I'm sure Ian here would be keen on that.
35	Ian	That's as may be but at present I'd rather confine this discussion to the immediate project in hand. I think the reporting relationships must be sorted out at your level.
36	David	Come on, Ian. You're fencing. Do you want to join the centre or not? I think it's important that we establish that.
37	Ian	Let's put it this way. I'm certainly glad that you've set up a centre here at HQ. I think it's got an important job of work to do. No doubt about that. On the other hand the management training team has been in existence for five or six years now, earning a reputation all over the company for sound, helpful work. That reputation has been hard won.
38	George	I think that's quite enough on this subject just now. I agree with Ian. It's something that you and I need to sort out, David, one day when the centre has established itself. Are we done then?
39	David	I wouldn't want to leave Ian and Chris with

the impression that we weren't at one on this one, George. I'm sure you agree that the amalgamation of the two units is highly desirable from the company's point of view? We have discussed this before and I thought that was our joint view?

40	George	Look! I thought I'd already made it clear that I don't want to discuss this now. In fact I'd go further, David, and say that I think it unfair of you to have introduced this without due warning. As far as we are concerned this meeting was convened to plan ways and means of introducing the MD's style to the rest of the company.
41	David	Very well. I can't help but comment that this is a pity in my view. We specifically had this issue of the centre and management training on our agenda. I feel that the plans for them to cooperate over the MD project lead us inevitably into discussion about the way the two units interface. To be prepared to discuss one and not the other is hardly logical. But still . . . if that's the way you want it.
42	George	Well, I'm off! I didn't think we were going to talk about this today. Got to be some-where else in a few minutes anyway . . .
43	David	Right. So long as we agree that it is important to work out the roles of the two units. We need to work together on a common charter. Close liaison to refine the boundaries is essential. No-one ever plans to duplicate you know. Duplication is always in the past tense. The danger is to leave these questions unanswered.
44	Ian	I'll get together with Chris then. Did we agree which of us was to lead the project?
45	Chris	Yes. I thought it was agreed that I should.
46	David	Fine. I look forward to hearing your proposals. An important project. No doubt

about that. The MD is a difficult man in many ways. If we can get people throughout the company adjusted to his thinking, blending their styles in with his . . . well, it'll make a vast difference . . . a vast difference.

Exit George and Ian

47	Fred	Well I don't know about you but I thought that was a difficult meeting in many ways.
48	David	Difficult? How do you mean? I thought we were pretty successful considering.
49	Chris	But I thought you said we weren't going to raise the question of amalgamation at this stage?
50	David	Well . . . the time seemed right. It's important to play these things by ear to some extent you know. I think it worked pretty well. We've got you appointed as project leader. What more do you want?
51	Chris	I didn't get the impression that Ian was particularly happy about that.
52	David	Oh come on now! It's all been agreed. You've had a lot of my time this afternoon already . . .
53	Fred	Come on Chris. David has had enough of us for now. We'll sort ourselves out all right later.

Once again David has largely failed to achieve the objective that we decided to analyse his performance against. The main responsibilities of ODC and MTU have not been listed or even talked through; he never made it clear that he didn't favour amalgamation — indeed George and Ian obviously got the impression that he did! Neither George nor Ian left the meeting remarking that it had been useful. Quite the reverse in fact; George seemed rather peeved. The only fragment of success is that there was agreement from Ian to work with Chris on the MD project (31 and 44) but each time the agreement looked rather half baked and short of anything resembling enthusiasm as Chris pointed out in 51.

Now it is quite possible that we have misunderstood David's objective for the meeting. People's objectives are not visible unless they choose to make them so by *saying* what they are. The 'evidence' for David's objective came in the earlier discussion with Chris and Fred (Chapter 2, page 37 contributions 33, 35 and 38) but it may well be that he had hidden objectives that were more influential in shaping his behaviour than the one we are using. If so, notice the effect that his behaviour had. In the main he was instrumental in causing considerable confusion and, by the time George and Ian had left, Fred and Chris both admit to seeing difficulties. David, on the other hand, is either happy because his hidden objective had been achieved or is rationalizing his failure away (48, 50 and 52). This is a frequent ritual that people go through after interactions and it is made easier if they do not disclose their objective until *after* the event. This means that whatever the outcome they can adjust their objective to fit and, accordingly, can guarantee success every time. It looks as if David is a skilled rationalizer!

Despite this let us apply our in and out of step criterion to David's behaviour using the objective we, in our wisdom, dreamed up on his behalf! During the time that George and Ian were present David produced 18 contributions. My analysis breaks down his behaviour into six main clusters as follows:

1,3

David's starter behaviours. In the event 3 was particularly unfortunate because it gave George and Ian 'the floor' so to speak. This wouldn't have mattered except that it revealed a total misunderstanding about the objective for the meeting; 3 was out of step with David's objective. He would have done better to start with some sort of declaration of his objective and to have taken it from there. This would have brought the misunderstanding into the open from the outset and they could have done a deal: you help me to achieve my objective and I will help you to achieve yours.

7, 11, 13, 15
All out of step with David's objective but in step with George and Ian's. These behaviours could be forgiven if, subsequently, David had managed to get back in step with his own objective.

20, 24, 26
Possibly in step with the part of his objective to do with securing a commitment to cooperation. But it is rather an obscure way of trying to achieve the objective and certainly causes Chris's resentment (22 and 25) and Ian's bid to secure clarity (27, 31 and 44). On balance, I will credit David with these behaviours and judge them to be more in step than out of step.

28, 30
Out of step because the spirit of the objective was very much to do with sorting things out in some detail there and then, within the compass of the meeting.

32, 34, 36, 39, 41
As out of step as out of step can be! The slide starts innocently enough with David's remark in 32 but, by the time he responds to George in 34 he has completely broken step with his own objective. A classic case of failing to control behaviour so that it aligns adequately with the objective.

43, 46
A feeble attempt at recovery but still out of step for the same reason that 28 and 30 were. David is shunting the detailed work on defining the responsibilities of the two units out of the meeting when his objectives clearly envisaged that this would be a legitimate activity at the meeting.

Overall then, my score sheet has a maximum of four of David's contributions in step (1, 20, 24 and 26), and I am hesitant about those, and the remaining 14 out of step. A poor behavioural performance that did nothing to avert failure.

SECOND CASE STUDY

This time the transcript that follows gives a verbatim account of an appraisal discussion between two men. They work in a large company's public relations department. Len is public relations director and he is appraising Bob, who is one of his direct subordinates. They have worked together for many years and so tend to have a casual, friendly relationship. As you will see, Len is new to appraisal discussions in the more formal sense.

Please centre attention on Len's behaviour and again to see how well it fits with the following objective:

Len's objective: to have appraised Bob's performance in such a way that at least one plan for improved performance is agreed. Len will have been successful if:

- At least one of the plans tightens up on the procedure for getting publicity in the provincial press throughout the country
- All the plans for improvement are in specific enough 'action' terms to leave them in no doubt about what has to be done and by whom in future
- Bob comes up with at least one plan for improvement himself
- Bob indicates that he has found the appraisal discussion useful/helpful
- He (Len) learns something about how he could improve his own performance as departmental head.

With this objective as the backcloth analyse Len's behaviour in the transcript.

> *Len and Bob have been talking for some time about other matters when . . .*

1 Len   Well that just about wraps that up then, Bob. Have you anything else to add?

2	Bob	No, no . . . I'm quite clear about that. Leave it to me.
3	Len	Fine. Er . . . Bob, you know this appraisal scheme they've been pushing lately?
4	Bob	Yes. I went to one of the presentations. It seemed like a good idea. Of course it isn't as applicable in our sort of work. But in principle I welcomed it.
5	Len	How do you mean? What sort of work is it applicable to then?
6	Bob	Oh I'd have thought it was more useful in departments where the work is . . . you know, more tangible or more measurable.
7	Len	Don't you think it's possible to put measures on our own activity then, Bob?
8	Bob	Well, it depends what you mean by measures doesn't it? If you mean objective things like how frequently we get favourable mentions in the press or the customer complaint levels, things like that, well, they are just trivial aren't they? Missing the essence of the thing.
9	Len	Hmm. I'm not so sure. Take the money back guarantee launch. We agreed to get wide coverage in provincial newspapers throughout the country as well as all the TV and national press coverage. How well did we do on that?
10	Bob	Well of course the TV and national press coverage was admitted to be about the best we've ever had.
11	Len	I know, I know. But I'm asking about our success in getting *local* coverage. If you remember, less glamorous provincial plugs were reckoned to be a key factor in getting people throughout the country to come and book through us.
12	Bob	Yes, well, off hand I'm not sure how we faired locally. We didn't really set up a scheme to monitor local press coverage did we?
13	Len	Didn't we? I thought that was implicit in that part of the plan.

14	Bob	Just a minute. Are you *getting* at me? Is this supposed to be an appraisal interview?
15	Len	Well, yes. I must admit that I thought we would have a chat about your . . . our . . . performance. I hoped you might think it a good idea.
16	Bob	But we've been together for seven years now and you've never had occasion to criticize me during that time.
17	Len	I'm not criticizing you. If I've understood it right, appraising isn't so much about criticizing as about helping. I'm only raising the matter of the failure to get sufficient local press coverage in order to help improve future performance.
18	Bob	Well, I'm sorry Len, but I resent this. I didn't know this was to be an appraisal discussion, otherwise I would have prepared myself. It seems quite unfair for you to suddenly launch into a premeditated attack and expect me to defend myself. If that's what appraisal is about let's forget it and go back to our normal way of carrying on.
19	Len	Look, Bob, I've clearly not handled the opening of this session at all well. I didn't want to have you up in arms, quite the contrary in fact. I was keen to keep this as informal and casual as possible.
20	Bob	Maybe I have over reacted a bit. It just seems a bit much to launch into an appraisal discussion after seven years working closely together without any warning.
21	Len	Okay, Bob, I'm sorry about that. Must admit I felt a bit embarrassed about the whole thing. But it's policy now you know, and anyway I've been thinking about this appraisal business and it certainly seems to make sense. It's made me realize that I've been rather remiss in the past. Not giving people enough explicit feedback

and help. Just being prepared to muddle along with half understandings and vague objectives.

22 Bob I see what you are getting at. I've never had any trouble being clear about my objectives personally and I always feel that we understand each other pretty well, but other people in the department do complain that they have trouble being certain about what it is you want them to do precisely. Oh! I mustn't exaggerate, it doesn't come up all that often.

23 Len Often enough to explain some of my disappointments with people's performance I bet.

24 Bob How do you mean?

25 Len Well let's go back to the example we were talking about earlier Bob. When we agreed to go for wide coverage in the local press as well as nationally, I obviously *expected* certain things to happen. In the event they didn't happen or, at least, I don't think they did. So whose fault would you say that was?

26 Bob I'm still very surprised that you keep bringing that up, Len. You had better come clean about what it was that you expected to happen, that didn't. I thought we'd done a good job on the money back guarantee scheme. It's widely acknowledged that we did anyway.

27 Len How about us doing it the other way round? If you'll tell me exactly what was done to ensure wide coverage in local papers, I'll promise to come clean about my disappointments.

28 Bob Okay, Len. Well as you know our resources were pretty strained doing all the liaising with the national and trade press. Those press conferences take some organizing.

29 Len You're stalling again Bob!

30 Bob Oh all right. I admit that I didn't think the local press campaign was anything like top priority. What difference would local coverage really have made anyway?

31	Len	So, what *was* done Bob?
32	Bob	Well, I think we sent out a memo to each of the branch managers urging them to push it with the local press in their respective areas.
33	Len	A memo or a press release? Did we put 'copy' into their hands?
34	Bob	Just a memo I think. I expected the branch managers to see the advantages of getting local coverage in whatever way they thought appropriate. It's very difficult for us to know what makes attractive copy for the local press. It varies enormously from area to area.
35	Len	Have we followed up to see how many branch managers *did* see the advantages?
36	Bob	No. I admit we haven't got round to that yet. Anyway, surely it was up to them? *They* were free to push it or not as they felt fit?
37	Len	You agree that one of our objectives was to get wide local press coverage in the launch programme?
38	Bob	Yes. A low priority one perhaps, but it was listed, yes.
39	Len	So the question is, is it reasonable or even professional for us to simply delegate the actions necessary to achieve one of *our* objectives to the retail branch managers?
40	Bob	Just another example of bumph from head office you mean?
41	Len	Partly, partly. Look Bob, I know you're short staffed down there but, in retrospect, what steps do you think you ought to have taken in the achievement of that objective?
42	Bob	We should have sent out a press release I suppose. Then if the branch manager was busy or didn't feel like going to a lot of extra trouble, at least he could have passed the press release to the right quarter and left it at that.
43	Len	Yes I'm sure that would have been preferable. Branch managers just haven't got time to write their own copy. That's an example of how we

as a department are supposed to help them isn't it?

44 Bob Can't argue about that one, Len. That's obviously quite right.

45 Len Could we agree that in future whenever we try to co-ordinate press coverage via line managers of any kind, we always take it upon ourselves to provide the copy?

46 Bob Sure, yes. We should be doing that anyway.

47 Len So that can be adopted as a *measurable* aspect of future performance can it, Bob?

48 Bob Hmm. I see what you're getting at.

49 Len I'm sure it's just a question of basic communications between us. If we can't communicate clearly in this the PR department I don't see much hope for us!

50 Bob But talking of communications between us Len, I was wondering . . .

51 Len Wondering what Bob? If you've got any suggestions that'll help please let's have them. It's all part of the appraisal after all.

52 Bob Well, I was wondering if you and I could spend longer at the outset of a project, defining it more precisely, allocating priorities, deciding who is going to do what and so on. I honestly didn't realize that you thought provincial coverage on the guarantee project as important as you obviously did. Somehow there was a misunderstanding between us on that one, Len.

53 Len Hmm. We'll have to be careful that I don't finish up doing your job for you.

54 Bob No, no it's not that. Suppose for example we worked together, just at the start of new projects on setting the objectives. Once they have been agreed between us I'd expect to go off and decide on the best methods etc to get the job done properly.

55 Len Yes. I see what you mean, that's back to objectives and measures again isn't it? You're

suggesting that we fashion the objectives and standards *together*, so that we have complete understanding then leave you to get on with the job within the agreed constraints?

56 Bob Exactly! I'd certainly be happier if we went about it that way. You see, we do things so informally at the moment, I'm sure we leave lots unsaid that should be said. Think how often it transpires that I thought you were going to do something and you thought I was . . . it's a muddle.

57 Len Okay. Let's leave it at that then. Let's agree that we'll use the new system for all future projects and that the onus is on you to come with some starter objectives and keep pinning me down till you're clear enough.

58 Bob Right Len, so long as you don't mind. Must admit that I've often wanted to do that but I thought you'd take offence to be quite honest.

59 Len Perhaps this shows us the value of having these appraisal discussions. It certainly helps to direct attention on things like communication problems doesn't it? Usually we're too busy with the job in hand to consider these other issues. But they're important aren't they?

60 Bob They certainly are. In fact it's difficult to separate them out from the job itself. Obviously *how* you set the project up with me, the objectives we agree and so on are vital elements in determining its success, aren't they?

61 Len We are agreed then. I hope you didn't think I was being too critical earlier on, Bob? Overall I think you know that I know you do a good professional job. I certainly wouldn't want this discussion to have given you a different impression.

62 Bob No, no. I'm glad we've talked like this in fact, I must say this appraisal business seems more

applicable to us than I thought at first. Very useful, really very useful.

By my reckoning Len has been successful in achieving the objective. He got the issue of press releases for provincial papers thoroughly aired and agreed. (Bob's behaviour in 42 and 44 for example); Bob explicitly comments on the usefulness of the discussion (62) and comes up with a suggestion for improvement himself (52). Furthermore, the discussion has resulted in Len learning about an improvement area for his own performance (55 and 57). All in all, a perfect match between the objective and the outcome.

So Len has been successful in achieving his ends. Now let us look at the means he employed. Here is my in step, out of step analysis starting with 3 since contributions 1 and 2 are the tailpiece of the last interaction and not relevant to the appraisal.

3, 5, 7, 9, 11, 13
These must be judged a very oblique opening to the appraisal. They are in step with the part of the objective to do with press releases for the provinces but out of step with other parts of the objective that call for the appraisal discussion to be openly acknowledged as such. For example, it is difficult to see how Len hoped to get Bob to comment favourably on the appraisal procedure if he (Bob) never knew that was what it was! On balance, Len opens with a string of out of step behaviours.

15, 17, 19, 21
This is the phase of the interaction where Len is forced, by Bob's behaviour, to 'come clean' about it being an appraisal! In a sense, these are 'changing step' behaviours that result in Len adjusting his behaviour sufficiently to be fully in step by 21. On balance, Len's behaviour in this part of the exchange was in step but only because Bob forced the issue.

23–49
Fourteen consecutive behaviours all nicely in step with the objective culminating in specific agreement between the two men.

51, 53, 55, 57
The phase of the discussion where the tables are turned and Bob produces his suggestion aimed at improving Len's behaviour. My only out of step query is 53 which I consider a risky behaviour in the light of the fact that Len wanted to learn something to his own advantage. His reaction in 53 could have dampened the suggestion down rather than encouraged it. In the event Bob pressed his point home and Len got back in step again by 55.

59, 61
Rounding off behaviours by Len, both in step with the part of his objective to do with giving Bob a good feeling about it all.

In summary, Len was very successful in achieving his objective and deservedly so, since out of a total of 30 behaviours, 23 were completely in step. Only the opening sequence, where Len tried to manipulate Bob into an appraisal discussion in a very indirect way, was out of step together with a momentary lapse in 53.

SUMMARY

We have looked at two interactions in a bid to clarify the links between behaviour and objectives. The first was an example of an ends and means failure; the second was a success on both counts.

This sort of analysis has shown that it is possible to think of behaviour in terms of its in or out of stepness with objectives provided the objectives are specific enough. The next chapter concentrates attention on objectives since they are the pivot on which behaviour rotates.

One last point before we move on: the case studies we have looked at so far could lead you to conclude that means and ends always go hand in hand together with a sort of inevitable correlation between the two. Alas, this is not so. It is quite possible to fail to achieve your ends even though your behaviour throughout the interaction was totally compatible with the objective. It is also possible for your objective to be realized quite fortuitously when predominantly out of step behaviours have been used. This is because behaviour is only one factor among many that determine success or failure. Interactive skill is all about arranging behaviour so that we increase the *probability* of being successful. There are no guarantees that it will always work.

4 Developing realistic objectives

As a subject matter objectives are undoubtedly a bore. At best they are a discipline forcing us to specify things clearly and precisely. At worst, they are an uncomfortable threat. I have noticed with some sympathy the lengths to which people will go to avoid the business of defining objectives. Common comments are:

'It isn't possible to set precise objectives in our sort of work of course. We have to play things largely by ear.'

'Objectives don't make any difference to what we do on a day to day basis. Just because we write down an objective it doesn't change anything.'

'Objectives? Yes, I've got some somewhere in this drawer . . . I think . . .'

'Objectives are just a nasty way of pinning people down and depriving them of initiative.'

'Objectives spoil our fun. We enjoy 'fire fighting', reacting to situations, never knowing what is going to happen next. They take the thrill out of spontaneity. They aren't natural.'

It is really tragic that objectives, by and large, are so misunderstood and have such a jaded reputation — tragic but inevitable. The process of working out objectives *is* inherently tedious. The discipline of writing objectives down is just that — a discipline. And, when all is said and done, objectives in themselves *don't* change anything. They require *activity*, in the form of plans and actions to bring them to life. Since activity is necessary, with or without objectives, many people conclude that objectives are an optional extra they can happily dispense with.

The *intellectual* case for objectives is, however, strong. It can be argued it is not a question of deciding whether to have objectives or not. There is not an either-or choice. Man is a purposeful animal and as such he *always* has objectives. The only choice we have is whether to fashion the objectives that are there anyway, into a form where they can be articulated.

The skills involved in making objectives conscious and capable of articulation are our primary concern in this chapter. As we saw in chapter 2, objectives occupy a central role in interactive skills since they form the vital bridge between situations and behaviour itself. Before going on to look at the mechanics of working out objectives, let me put the case for bothering at all.

Research shows that a typical manager spends something like 80 per cent of his time in face to face interaction with people as a legitimate part of his job. Many of them don't *feel* it is legitimate as revealed when they say things like: 'I get into the office early so that I can get on with some *real* work before the interruptions start.' Or, 'What a day! Non-stop meetings and nothing achieved. I'll have to take all this work home with me.' I have an idea that the attitude that interacting is not really working is the key to understanding why acceptance of sloppy, shapeless rambling interactions is so widespread. Paradoxically, it may be precisely *because* our expectations are set so low that we feel interactions are destined to remain this way and are somehow immune to significant improvement. On the whole I have found managers to be amazed at the notion that interactions, and not just grander, longer-term activities, benefit from having precise objectives. I have stopped managers in mid-interactive flight, as it were, and asked them to tell me what their objectives for the current interaction were. I know of no surer way of reducing them to hesitant 'umming and urring'! In my experience people are much clearer about their 'middle distance' objectives, six months and one year hence, than they are about their immediate, here and now ones. Yet 80 per cent of time is absorbed in interactions of one sort or another; big and small ones, formal and informal ones. That is where, day by day, both time and effort go. Taken singly, therefore, each interaction may seem of insufficient consequence to go to the trouble to have conscious objectives and the other accompanying paraphernalia. Taken collectively, however, interactions are where productivity can easily hit an all time low. Accordingly, I believe that if anything *can* be done to improve the quality and productivity of interactions it would be a really significant contribution. Having conscious objectives for interactions is part of the answer. Behaving properly, in accordance with the objectives, is the other part.

WHAT IS AN OBJECTIVE?

An objective is a prediction about the state of affairs that you wish to exist at some specified time in the future. An objective is always arrived at by making a judgement about how much it is reasonable to achieve in a given period.

The way people make this judgement differs considerably from individual to individual. Some are brave and risk committing themselves to an enormously challenging objective on a flimsy data base. Others are much more cautious. They wait longer before taking the plunge. They assemble as much information about the situation as they can. They hedge their bets by building 'either or' type escape clauses into the objective. The *really* cautious have two favourite ploys for protecting themselves against being wrong in their prediction. One is deliberately to leave the objective hazy and vague so that they have room for manoeuvre in claiming that subsequent events were in fact predicted accurately. In a group I often find that when someone says 'Oh come on! We are just playing with semantics. We all know what we mean' it is a sign that the rigours of defining a precise enough objective are proving too demanding. I have watched managers go to the very brink of defining a specific objective only to retreat back into the comfort of fudging the issue.

The other ploy, which some have developed into an accomplished game for survival, is to postpone the setting of the objective until either the eleventh hour before the event the objectives are supposed to predict or, if they are really smart, until *after* the event they are supposed to predict! This is a convenient way of always being right. No matter what happens you can claim that the outcome was the one you were aiming for!

These and other ploys miss the essence of what objectives are all about: making a sharp, precise prediction of the state of affairs which will exist, if you have been successful at a specified time in the future.

An objective is a statement articulating the outcome you want from a situation. The statement needs to be as specific and unambiguous as possible. It helps if the expression of the objective contains two elements. First, a nutshell description of the outcome you want. Secondly, some standards of success, so stated that they qualify any ambiguity in the nutshell description and can act, eventually, as practical indicators or measures of your success or failure.

Since in this book we are concentrating on face to face interactions our concern is quite properly going to be with how to set objectives for interactions of various kinds. In fact, the only difference between an objective for an interaction and any other sort of activity is purely one of longevity. The definition of an objective in the last paragraph is equally applicable whether we are talking about long-term objectives or short-term ones. A satisfactory articulation of intent contains the same basic ingredients.

Being able to distinguish between objectives occupying different time phases is a crucial skill if you are to be clear about the sorts of objectives it is realistic to go for in a thing like an interaction. As everyone knows interactions have fairly severe limits. The maxim 'when all is said and done, far more is said than done' rings very true. Interactions *are*, by their very nature, confined. The accent is usually on agreeing things, planning things and deciding things and rarely on actually *doing* things. The doing usually comes after, or in between, interactions.

Let us take an example to illustrate this. Suppose you are a manager with a group of staff who, on the whole, are a good bunch — with one exception. Your boss has asked you to take some action about this weak member within the next six months. What action you take is up to you. The man in question is always willing to undertake new work but somehow it never seems to get done precisely as you have asked or, more importantly, on time. He is always ready with the reasons, many of them very plausible, why it couldn't be done — afterwards!

Two weeks ago you asked him to prepare an important report for you. The matter was to be treated as urgent and the report should have been completed and received by you yesterday. It is only because you were hopelessly busy yourself yesterday that you didn't check up on its whereabouts. Now the subordinate has asked to see you to complain about being overloaded with work. You have to find some way of dealing with the immediate problems as well as making some progress in improving his longer-term performance. You can only spare one hour before having to keep another appointment.

That then is the situation. The problem is now to decide how much it is desirable and realistic to achieve in the interaction with your subordinate. Here are a few of the choices that face you:

- To have explored his complaint about being over-worked and convinced him that it was unfounded
- To have reviewed progress on the missing report and committed him to completion by (a time acceptable to you in the light of the work that remained to be done on it and its urgency)
- To have appraised his overall performance and produced an action plan aimed at making him more reliable
- To have improved his performance so that he always gets work done to the standards set and completed on time.

Apart from variations in detail one of the most significant differences between these four possibilities is in terms of their ambitiousness. The first one doesn't push the issue nearly as far as the second. The second doesn't push it as far as the third and so on. They represent very different judgements about how far it is realistic to go within the time span of the interaction. This judgement is important because it is fundamental in predisposing the outcome. If you decide to aim for the fourth objective, for example, you will fail simply because it expresses a level of achievement far in excess of anything that could be accomplished in one inter-action. The fourth objective may well be an expression of what you are *ultimately* aiming at, but knowing that isn't likely to leave you much clearer about what to strive to achieve in the immediate interaction.

Then again, if you decide to go for the third objective you may also fail simply because one hour is unlikely to be long enough for this level of accomplishment. On the other hand, if you go for the first you may succeed totally but that might strike you as 'cold comfort' since the first objective pinpoints an inadequate success in the context of the missing report and the subordinate's persistent performance problems.

It is often easier to recognize 'wrong' objectives than it is to be definitive about which are 'right'. What is 'right' in part depends on your own skills as a participant in the situation. It *is* possible to say, however, that the objective you set should always be:

in step with your analysis of the situation

realistic in the sense that you judge it is genuinely possible to be successful

challenging in the sense that being successful isn't a near certainty but will have to be earned.

Just to round off the earlier example, but not to pretend to give the only or 'right' answer, here is the objective that I would aim for in my interaction with the subordinate:

To have produced a plan that he can adhere to to prevent him taking on work that he can't get done on time.

I will have been successful if:

- The plan is specific enough such that he can run through the 'drill' he has to follow without me having to correct him significantly
- He will have suggested more of the content of the plan than I have had to
- He will thank me for having helped to solve his problem
- He will offer to produce the missing report by a time that I consider reasonable in the light of the fact that it is already a day late and is urgent.

THE BENEFITS OF SETTING OBJECTIVES FOR INTERACTIONS

There are really three interrelated benefits to be reaped by having clear, precise objectives when interacting.

First, the objective helps you to be clear about what you have to *do* in a bid to get it to come true. It is amazing to me how few people seem to have made the conceptual leap from objectives to activities. Indeed, many find it difficult to distinguish between the two and more about that in the next section when we look at some of the pitfalls to avoid when setting objectives. Too often the objective is viewed as a rather troublesome thing that needs minimal maintenance like updating it now and again. In fact living, as opposed to dead, objectives continually influence all activities that follow in their wake. Decisions and plans need to be made in the light of the objective. For example, the objective helps to shape your behaviour. Conscious knowledge of the objective means that you can spot, and even curb, irrelevancies and be better at controlling your behaviour so that it contributes to its achievement. Subsequent chapters on planning and shaping behaviour will expand on these activities but always against the backcloth of objectives themselves.

A second benefit in having clear, precise objectives is that it makes it easy to compare the actual outcome with your prediction. This means you can be quite certain about total success, relative success, failure and so on. This, in turn, means that you are in a better position to learn from experience. During a programme I was running recently, this emphasis on consciously monitoring performance and learning from experience became encapsulated in the group's *modus operandi* to such an extent that whenever they 'failed' they would chant 'There's no such thing as failure: only opportunities to learn!' Without objectives you can never quite be sure about how to view the outcome and this is especially true of interactions. It is so easy to muddle through, sliding from one interaction to the next with no sharp concept of the degree of success you are attaining. And remember that for most of us something like 80 per cent of our working time can be absorbed in this way.

Finally the third benefit is that, if you consciously have an objective in mind, it helps you to communicate to others what you want to achieve. If you yourself aren't too sure of your objective, you aren't in a position to decide whether to reveal it to others or not. Saying what your objectives are in interaction is only possible if they are in a form that makes their articulation possible. I believe that interactions often meander on in their fuzzy way precisely because participants are literally lost for words in describing what they wish to achieve. This leads to all sorts of weird goings-on like, for example, spending a whole interaction discovering, through a sea of innuendos, that the parties involved have substantially different objectives. This discovery need not have been so tortuous if the objectives had been in a communicable form. In fact, differences could have been established within the first ten minutes. I am not suggesting that explicitly declaring your objectives is any sort of golden rule but it is surprising how often simply *saying* what your objectives are is entirely compatible with making it as likely as possible that they will be achieved.

There are other benefits in setting objectives but I hope these three are appealing enough to commend the approach to you.

SOME PITFALLS TO AVOID WHEN SETTING OBJECTIVES

There are four particular pitfalls to avoid when setting objectives. The first is much more difficult to pinpoint in cold print than the other three, which are much more mechanistic.

The first hazard is to avoid having objectives that only have tenuous links with the situation itself. This is really the in step, out of step concept over again except that this time it relates to the bonding between situations and objectives rather than between objectives and behaviour. The pitfall is to pay only cursory attention to the factors that comprise the situation and, in consequence, to set objectives that do not really fit the circumstances. In practice, the objective should cascade out of your understanding of the situation in a fairly effortless way. The more you have to work away contriving it, the less likely it is to dovetail with the real situation. The acid test is to imagine that someone is going to audit your objective and demand to know how each part relates to the situation. If you can satisfy the auditor that each bit of the objective is in step with the situation, then you have survived the first hazard.

The second hazard is to have overall objectives instead of end of interaction ones. Going into an interaction with objectives like 'To make a profit', 'To cut the incidence of industrial action by 50 per cent', 'To improve Bill's managerial performance' is totally inadequate. These are longer-term, or overall, objectives that cannot possibly be achieved within the life-span of an interaction. Certainly it is of the utmost importance to be aware of the overall objective. For one thing we need to know it in order to mesh the step-by-step, interaction by interaction, activity by activity objectives in with it. But overall objectives are not adequate in guiding us satisfactorily through interactions that, remember, can take up to 80 per cent of our time. We must have shorter-term objectives to guide us through here-and-now happenings like interactions. For example, the problem with having an objective like 'To improve Bill's managerial performance' is that it is unlikely to be achieved just by a single interaction with him.

There is more to it than that! To be clear about how much to achieve in an interaction with Bill, we need to backtrack from this expression of an overall objective. Judgements about what it is reasonable to go for by the end of the interaction will vary, but for the sake of this example let us say that the immediate objective could be 'To agree criteria for judging Bill's performance as a manager'. Let us freeze the example there for a minute and return to it when we have considered the third pitfall.

The third hazard when setting objectives is not specifying standards of success. Earlier we defined an objective as: 'a statement articulating the outcome you desire from a situation. The statement needs to be specific and as unam-biguous as possible. It helps if the objective contains two elements: first, a nutshell description of the outcome you desire, secondly, some standards of success, so stated that they qualify any ambiguity in the nutshell description and can act as practical indicators, or measures of your success or failure'.

If we merely have the 'nutshell description' as our end-of-interaction objective we are nearly back to the perils we have just been discussing when having overall objectives as a replacement for more immediate ones. The problem is that we have left ourselves too much room for manoeuvre. This may seem an advantage rather than a snag except that it means we deny ourselves at least two out of the three benefits described on pages 63 to 64. You cannot be sufficiently clear what you have to *do* to accomplish the objective if it is vague. You are also hard put to it (except by rationalizing) to assess the extent of your success or failure.

The answer is to spice up the prediction by including standards of success as an integral part of the objective. Without them we are just playing at predicting in the same way that a soothsayer might when couching forecasts in such vague terms that whatever happens is bound to compare favourably with it. Specifying standards of success forces us to take the nutshell statement and tighten it up. Standards might be set in some, or all, of the following areas:

The amount of work that will have been accomplished by the end of the interaction if it is to be judged a success

The quality of work that will have been done by the end of the interaction

The behaviour that the other person, or persons, will have displayed by the end of the interaction if it is to be judged a success. Including behavioural standards is vital since behaviour is the visible aspect. How someone reacts in interaction is a vital indicator to how they are likely to behave after it

The time it will have taken to accomplish the end-of-interaction objective.

In order to exemplify these let us return to the example we started earlier about improving Bill's managerial performance.

If you remember, we shrunk this overall objective down into the immediate one of having a session with Bill where we would 'agree the criteria for judging Bill's performance as a manager'. Possible standards of success might be:

— For the amount of work: 'We will have produced at least six criteria'

— For the quality of work: 'The criteria will be in writing and each will be specific enough to make it possible for Bill and me to judge his performance against it without hesitation and interpolation and, in so doing, to reach the same conclusion'

— For behaviour:
  'Bill will have spontaneously suggested at least half the criteria'
  'Bill will have spontaneously remarked that the session has helped him to be clear about what is involved in being a good manager'

'Bill will volunteer to get the criteria typed out with a copy for me'
'Bill will be able to run through the criteria (in his own words) without leaving any out and without it being necessary for me to 'correct' him because of any difference in understanding between us'

— For time: 'Not more than one hour'.

If you feel uncertain about how to articulate standards of this kind try the exercises towards the end of this chapter on page 70. There are six different situations for which to analyse and set end-of-interaction objectives. You might also look back at the sample objectives we were using as our backcloth in the earlier exercises to do with judging the in or out of step relationship with behaviour. The essential point about standards is that the sharper and more precise your definition of success can be, short of becoming hair splitting, the easier it is to shape activities and behaviour accordingly.

The final hazard to mention in this section relates back to some earlier points made about the need to distinguish between objectives and activities. In teaching circles it is the difference between reading a Shakespeare play and what the teacher wants the pupil to get out of reading it. The former is an activity, the latter the objective. Returning to our example, therefore, we could list a number of activities but their sum total does not amount to the end-of-interaction objective. The objective should be a 'snapshot' prediction, capturing the state of affairs we want to exist by the end of the interaction. The activities, on the other hand, are the ongoing plan, or agenda, we shall use to guide us through the interaction. For example, we might list the following activities as part of the plan for our interaction with Bill:

To get him to admit that he has some problems in managing properly
To establish why he finds it difficult to manage

To convince him that having some explicit criteria might help

To produce the list of criteria

This sort of 'shopping list' is not an end-of-interaction objective. Contrast it with the objective developed earlier on pages 67–8. Notice that only the last activity in our chronological listing of activity comes close to the objective we set. This underlines the vital fact that the objective should be concerned with defining the end point of the interaction and not be confused with the plan for how to proceed towards that end point.

In conclusion can I say that setting 'good' objectives that compare favourably with the definition is not easy, but we have to practise it if we are to qualify for the benefits discussed earlier. The discipline of thinking through objectives to a sufficient level of specificity is rejected by many people as too onerous. In my experience, however, people who *have* trained themselves, quite literally, to *live*-by-objectives have gained a whole new perspective in their lives besides becoming more effective in their people-transactions. Objectives certainly 'beef-up' interactions that would otherwise be unrewarding and routine.

People who have had bad experiences with objectives, and there are plenty of casualties, often insist that they should not be bound by specific objectives but should feel free to take up whatever happens to be of interest at the moment. Objectives, they say, confine them to a narrow prescribed route and blind them to alternative, perhaps more appropriate, courses of action. A good objective states an end point that can be achieved in many different ways. *How* we got Bill to join us in agreeing six criteria could have been done using a variety of different approaches. Ironically, concentrating on objectives instead of on the 'shopping list' agenda leaves us *free* to try new approaches. Rather than hamper creativity, objectives stimulate us to try new and more efficient behavioural approaches. In any case, objectives need not be immutable. New standards can be added and old ones discarded or changed. But it is important to accept that whenever we consciously modify an objective the need to do so is, in itself, an indictment of the judgements we have made in the light of the situation about what it was realistic to attempt. Of course we need to abandon an objective if, as the interaction unfolds, it strikes us as absurd and replace it with something more reasonable but this should not happen too frequently. Chopping and changing objectives is likely to make our behaviour appear as confusing as not having any objectives at all. The 'freedom', or spontaneity, that comes from no objectives, or vague ones, is largely illusory for it leaves us particularly susceptible to other people's objectives and vulnerable to any familiar routines. Objectives stimulate rather than hamper creativity.

EXERCISES IN SETTING REALISTIC OBJECTIVES FOR FACE TO FACE ENCOUNTERS

Here are six descriptions of different situations. They are only the bare bones and in each case you will need to make some assumptions in adding flesh to the bones. The idea is to work out what end-of-interaction objective you consider realistic and rigorous enough within the context of each situation. There are no right answers but, in order to give you a basis of comparison, I have written out my ideas on suitable objectives (they follow immediately after the chapter summary on page 74). If you do not wish to work your way through all six situations just try a couple. I recommend that you select the two which have the most similarity with the sort of everyday situations you are used to tackling.

Situation 1: Delegation problem
One of your subordinates has one real shortcoming: he will not delegate. Whenever there is any semblance of a crisis he goes in and does the job himself. When tackled on this he claims that his people respect him for being able to do a better job than they can or says that he likes 'to keep his hand in'. You suspect that his people resent these interventions whenever something is getting really interesting

and regard them as a vote of no confidence in their work. Furthermore, you have noticed that this inability or unwillingness to delegate results in your subordinate taking too much on himself. He frequently stays late to 'catch up' and increasingly fails to get jobs done to deadline. You decide that you have got to tackle this problem and get him to delegate more.

Situation 2: Procrastinating boss
Your boss is a renowned verbal rambler and procrastinator. You need a decision — urgently.

In 30 minutes a very good customer prospect is due to arrive to meet you. You have already had a series of meetings and things are looking good. Three days ago you had a session with your boss when you asked if you might make some concession to this prospective customer which you are sure will clinch the deal. You didn't bother him with precise details of the concessions you expect are necessary — you were more interested in getting his blessing in principle with some guidance about how much room for manoeuvre you were permitted.

You have already chased him twice since then for a decision. Once he said he was still thinking about it and the second time he was just rushing off to some meeting or other. You are now going to see him to try to get a decision and you predict that he will not have made his mind up and will still be 'worrying' about it.

Situation 3: Taking over new departments
You have just been appointed departmental manager of a newly formed department. Your department contains three branches. One of them you know intimately, having run it yourself for three years. It is now run by one of the people in that branch with whom you worked closely and successfully. The two other branches are a service branch which you never used or thought much of before and a branch selling a fairly technical product direct to the customer. You are not familiar with either the product or with operating in a customer revenue environment.

The branch from which you came is in many ways more

advanced in its work than the other two. Its staff are on average higher paid, for instance, and its 'specialness' has been known to cause resentment.

You only know the two branch managers to say 'hello' to and you are anxious to get off to a good start with them both. So you have arranged to meet them one at a time, for an initial 'getting to know each other' couple of hours.

Situation 4: The ideas woman
You have a colleague with whom you have worked on a number of projects in the past. You know her as someone who is always coming up with ideas, some good, some mediocre and some appalling. She seems to go for quantity of ideas and to let other people worry about quality. This has not earned her a very good reputation since the work 'culture' seems to put a higher premium on good ideas rather than a lot of ideas.

She has sent you a draft of a new idea she has had, worked out in enormous detail. She wants to come and discuss it with you as somebody whose views are important to her, not as somebody who will be involved in any future implementation of the idea. Unfortunately, you think the idea is completely unworkable in its present form, although you recognize there is a germ of value in it.

She respects your opinion. You hope to steer her away from making a fool of herself without losing her respect.

Situation 5: Activity diaries
You have to brief a group of your subordinates on the part they are to play in a nationwide exercise to obtain information about how they spend their working time. It involves them in keeping an activity diary each day for a month: a laborious and unrewarding task.

You are experiencing some irritation as it is not long since a similar request was made. No-one, including you, heard the outcome of the previous study and several doubted its necessity.

You have put it on the agenda of a meeting you are due to have with all your subordinates and you wonder how you can break the news of this imposed chore and get enough commitment from them at the same time.

Situation 6: Salesman's expenses
You are an area sales manager appointed just six months ago. One of your best salesmen, with an extremely good record, is inclined to 'swing' quite a lot of his expenses. He is on a basic salary plus bonus system and his earnings are substantial. You were shocked by the level of these expenses from the start but approved the claim for the first two months without querying anything with him. You knew this was sheer cowardice at the time but hoped the situation would resolve itself. It didn't and so in the third month you spoke to him about the high level of his expenses. He was sullen but agreed to watch them. Since then you have not been able to detect the slightest change.

You are about to meet him to take up the matter of expenses for the second time. You expect him to feel that his good sales record more than justifies the level of expenses and to see you as being unnecessarily petty in raising the matter again.

SUMMARY

The chapter has concentrated on objectives. It started by admitting to their unpopularity but, despite this, went on to look at the benefits they bring and what was involved in making objectives conscious and capable of articulation.

A number of reasons were advanced in support of objectives. We saw that even though each single interaction might seem of little consequence, collectively they can consume as much as 80 per cent of a manager's working time. Accordingly, three benefits were identified for having conscious objectives; that they help us to be clear about what activities are necessary; they make it easy to compare the actual outcome with the prediction; and finally, that if objectives are conscious then, if need be, they are declarable to others.

An objective was defined. In general terms objectives were described as predictions of the state of affairs that we wished to exist at some time in the future. More precisely, an objective was defined as a specific and unambiguous statement, articulating the outcome desired from a situation with standards pinpointing the acceptable level of success.

A number of common confusions it is easy to fall prey to were also examined. In summary these were: the perils of mistaking plans and activities for objectives; and finally, the hazard of leaving an objective vague and hazy without standards that describe the level of success required.

The chapter ended with the invitation to try your hand at setting realistic, end-of-interaction objectives for all, or some, of six descriptions of different situations. My own 'solutions' are given below.

SAMPLE OBJECTIVES FOR THE SIX SITUATIONS GIVEN ON PAGES 70–73

I must reiterate that these are not the only satisfactory 'solutions' to the situations given earlier. You could have substantially different ideas on suitable objectives and still be as 'right' as the ones given below. This is because, as we have seen throughout Chapter 4, setting objectives is a peculiarly personal affair. Judgements about what is realistic, about what is in step with the situation and, for that matter, about what is unambiguous, inevitably vary from person to person.

That understood, here are my thoughts on suitable objectives for each situation.

Situation 1: Delegation problem
To have produced a plan with X which sorts out which of the jobs he is currently doing himself can be given to someone else and identifies that person. The plan will also include what he can do to stop intervening in a crisis.

I shall have been successful if:

- The plan we have produced includes details on what, how, who, where and when

- The plan has allocated a minimum of four jobs which X is currently doing himself to someone else
- X has subscribed to the plan and said that it has been a helpful session. Also that he is going to action the plan
- X has himself suggested that sometime in the future there should be a further meeting to review the success of the plan and to make another one if necessary
- This has been achieved within two hours.

Situation 2: Procrastinating boss
To have got him to agree to all the concessions I am likely to need within 20 minutes.
I shall have been successful if I achieve this in such a way that:

- He will have shown no sign of resentment at being 'nagged' or pushed into a decision
- He will have shared the contribution rate with me to a maximum of 50 per cent
- He will have said that he is quite happy with the concession arrangement.

Situation 3: Taking over new departments
(For both branch managers in turn.) To have produced a list of items for our next working meeting together.
I shall have been successful if:

- The list has at least six items on it, all of which genuinely require both of us
- It has been produced in not less than one and not more than two hours
- He has contributed a minimum of half the items listed himself
- The date and time for the next meeting will have been agreed between us before we break up
- He has said that he looks forward to the next meeting in such a way that I'm inclined to think he really means it.

Situation 4: The ideas woman

To have got her to agree to a substantial rethink of her idea in order to make it workable.

I shall have been successful if:

- She has accepted that at least half of the difficulties I raise in relation to her idea *are* genuine snags
- She has said in her own words without any prompting from me, that she now sees that the 'culture' is geared to appreciate the quality as well as the quantity of ideas.
- She has told me that I've done her a big favour and asked if she might return at some later stage to check out the modified idea with me.
- This has been achieved in a maximum of one hour.

Situation 5: Activity diaries

To have got them to identify the benefits *to us* of keeping activity diaries and to have planned how to cash in on some of those benefits.

I shall have been successful if:

A minimum of half my subordinates have said that they agree that the benefits we have identified *are real* benefits.

Our plans do not cut across or interfere with the data head office needs from the activity records.

The plan we have produced includes the usual elements of how, who, where and when

Our plan will not be so ambitious that actioning it is likely to interfere with work, other than the normal interruption caused by keeping an activity record accurately for one month

I have judged that the plan, when actioned, will succeed in achieving 50 per cent of the identified benefits

This has been achieved in a maximum of two hours.

Situation 6: Salesman's expenses

To have got him to set a new standard of performance for himself which controls his level of expenses.

I shall have been successful if:

- He has set the standard, not me
- The standard he has set accords with my own ideas on a suitable level of expenses
- He has agreed that the standard will be binding for the next three months after which he will review it
- He has said that he now sees that a 'good' salesman is not just someone who brings in sales but someone who has a feel for his revenue to cost ratio
- This has been achieved within a maximum of one and a half hours.

5 How to analyse behaviour

It is time to let objectives slip into the background and to focus the limelight on behaviour once again. In the opening chapters we defined behaviour as everything we do which is overt and therefore immediately visible. One of the benefits of this definition, was that it meant that any aspect of behaviour could be observed and monitored in a straight-forward way, without the need for sweeping interpretations. In this chapter the concept is developed in much more detail together with some practical exercises aimed at improving your skill in doing a blow by blow analysis.

So far we have looked at behaviour in a rough and ready sort of way. Deciding whether a behaviour is in or out of step with objectives requires a *global* judgement. We now need to analyse behaviour much more carefully by breaking it down into smaller particles in order to understand the effects brought about by different behaviours.

The idea of breaking behaviour down into 'bits' and studying the interplay between them is not new. Indeed, worthwhile breakthroughs in the natural sciences usually have come as a result of painstaking attention to detail. The most obvious examples are to be found with studies into animal behaviour. In fact, if you read accounts of animal experiments the attention to detail may strike you as bordering on the neurotic. Drops of saliva are carefully counted, the rate of working levers and tread wheels is monitored on a 24 hour basis, the exact positions ducks take up on a lake is plotted on a grid by an army of observers, every hesitation a rat makes in finding its way through a maze is captured on film. In respectable experimental designs environmental variables are also controlled in minute detail so that changes in the behaviour can be associated with certain environmental conditions, not to others.

The same attention to detail rarely extends to human behaviour. Frequently this is because problems of human behaviour, delinquency and violence for example, are so pressing that public opinion has not the patience to let researchers start at square one. This sort of political and social pressure has meant that psychology has had a tough first 80 years trying to establish its credibility as a respectable science. Behavioural problems are on such a massive scale that the contrast between them with all their attendant urgency, and the plodding, micro, and often dispassionate research by psychologists seems intolerable. People demand to know 'What have experiments where subjects learn a list of nonsense syllables to do with increasing illiteracy?' 'What have those silly questions in intelligence tests to do with being successful in life?' 'What have interpretations of 'ink blots' to do with vandalism?'

There are similar risks of incurring your indignation when I suggest that one of the basic skills in interacting competently is that of analysing behaviour in some detail. We need some technique that breaks behaviour down into relevant but smaller particles than most of us are used to in everyday life. The technique I recommend was first used as a research tool but, particularly in the last twenty years, has enjoyed a revival as a method with practical pay-offs for us all.

In essence behaviour analysis is the process of breaking down behaviour into fairly specific 'bits' and labelling the bits with what are called behaviour categories. Since by definition any aspect of overt behaviour can be directly observed, it follows that all behaviours *can* be categorized. If we thought it useful, we could monitor eyelid movements, eyebrow twitches, finger strumming and head nodding and shaking. Again, making the important proviso *if we thought it useful*, we could monitor all sorts of verbal behaviours such as how frequently someone said 'you know', how often someone swore, how often someone's Rs sounded like Ws. But we are not going to be particularly concerned with any of these in this book and they are only used to reinforce the following points: that *any* behaviours are amenable to this analytical process; that behaviour analysis deals in relatively small 'bits'; and that choices about which 'bits' it is relevant to attend to are vitally important both from the point of view of practical expediency and of credibility for the technique. Monitoring eyebrow movements would neither be very useful nor credible in most managerial situations.

With behaviour analysis techniques we can take descriptions of behaviour at a more general 'styles' level and break them down into their constituent parts. Examples of 'style'-level descriptions are

'He is a very *demanding* boss'
'He seems so *aggressive*'
'He is a good *leader*'
'She strikes me as utterly *genuine*'
'He is rather *autocratic*'
'He is very *participative*'
'She is *determined*'
'He is an *entrepreneur*'

Descriptions like these are used hundreds of times each day. They are useful in everyday conversation but too ambiguous for planning purposes. The training manager, for example, wants to break down these styles into behavioural specifications so that he can design behaviour change programmes. The personnel manager, with the problem of advising on selection techniques, wants to translate vague notions about having business acumen or being an entrepreneur into behavioural skills that can be assessed in the selection process. And, much more important, *all of us* need to know how to arrange our behaviour so that we *are* determined, a good leader, genuine and so on. Time and time again I have been on behavioural science programmes where the invitation to experiment with different ways of behaving has been extended. The problem is how? What do I have to *do* to pull my behaviour out of its well worn ruts and try 'unnatural' alien behaviours? The invitation to change or experiment sounds plausible enough. Accepting it involves the skills of consciously arranging an outward display of certain behaviours and controlling the occurrence of others: the very *same* skills that we need if we are to be able to adjust behaviour so that it is in step with different objectives.

The 'secret', inasmuch as there is one, is to break style-level descriptions down into smaller behavioural bits. Our behaviour plan can then be built around the 'bits' instead of depending on vague intentions. Intentions are infamous for getting actioned less frequently than plans simply because intentions leave a yawning gap that only plans can bridge. *Intending* to get up early and do two hours work before breakfast is less likely to happen than if we plan to do it. Planning involves a series of action steps such as going to bed earlier than usual and setting the alarm or alarms. Planning behaviour is the subject of a later chapter. Our immediate concern in this one is to establish a technique for analysing behaviour.

Styles, then, are in effect, *conclusions* we reach about the way others operate. The conclusions are based on obser-vations of smaller behavioural 'bits'. Here are some examples.

Participative breaks down into the following behavioural 'bits':
Lots of seeking behaviours where the person explicitly asks for opinions, ideas, suggestions and proposals from others. The participative person also asks lots of questions of clari-fication and even puts his own ideas in the form of questions to people. When reacting to whatever suggestions and proposals are forthcoming, the participative person mainly supports and develops the ideas rather than squashing them.

Autocratic breaks down into the following behavioural 'bits':
Lots of telling and, proportionally, little asking. The auto-cratic person does not ask others for their ideas. He gener-ates lots of proposals and they rarely seem tentative or 'up

for discussion' but are more in the form of instructions or commands. Autocrats interrupt others when they are talking. On balance the autocratic person also mainly disagrees with, or points out the snags in other people's suggestions.

Determined breaks down into the following behavioural 'bits':
Answers questions without hesitation. Doesn't 'um and ur'. Speaks fast. Looks people straight in the eye.

Genuine breaks down into the following behavioural 'bits': Expresses feelings more than using factual-type information. Messages given by verbal behaviour do not differ from messages given by accompanying non-verbal behaviour (that is, you don't greet someone by saying 'I've been longing to meet you' with your head down, rummaging through a pile of papers!).

Clearly any style-level description is amenable to this sort of analysis by reversing the synthetic process that we all use to reach communicable conclusions about people. The danger in doing this is to break down styles into such fragmented 'bits' that synthesizing is impaired and we are unable to relate the 'bits' to the various styles. If I broke a cup into six pieces, for example, and displayed them, you could easily synthesize from the pieces to a whole cup. If, however, I pulverized the cup and showed you a heap of powder it is most unlikely that you could conclude it was once a cup. We must be careful not to pulverize behaviour styles. The whole point of a behaviour analysis technique is to become clearer about what is going on during a transaction. To do this we need analysis *and* synthesis.

BENEFITS OF BEHAVIOUR ANALYSIS

There are four interrelated benefits to be gained with a behaviour analysis approach. First, the behaviour categories give us a 'language' for describing what is happening, at a behavioural level, during interactions between people. The specificity of the language helps in making 'discoveries' about the importance of certain behaviours that might be missed at a more general descriptive level.

Secondly, the behaviour categories give us a practical means of consciously monitoring our own as well as other people's behaviour whenever we want to. Thirdly, the same behaviour categories can 'double' as a shorthand when thinking about how best to behave in the light of a particular situation and desired objective. Accordingly, the behaviour categories make it possible to plan and to control behaviour. Behaviour planning will be covered in Chapter 9. The final benefit is that behaviour analysis helps us to understand how to 'shape' other people's behaviour in response to our own. Behaviour shaping will be explored in Chapter 7.

INTRODUCTORY EXERCISE IN BEHAVIOURAL ANALYSIS

For the remainder of this chapter we shall concentrate on the first two benefits. Perhaps the best way to do this is to use a short transcript of people in interaction once again. Initially, all you need do is read it through to get a general impression of what is happening and how the participants are behaving.

This is a transcript of part of a meeting between five managers.

1 Frank   Right, let's make a start.

2 Sheila   Before we begin on the items listed on this agenda, could I raise another matter?

3 Frank   I find it hard to imagine what can be so urgent that it isn't already on the agenda or, alternatively, can't wait until Any Other Business.

4 Sheila   My reason for bringing it up now was that I hoped my suggestion would have an immediate pay off; whereas if I held it until . . .

5	Frank	. . . All right. Let's hear your suggestion and *then* decide whether to deal with it straight away or slot it in somewhere else.
6	Tony	Good idea, Frank.
7	Bill	I can see we are going to finish late again.
8	Sheila	Oh, I don't think this will take long. I just want to suggest that since the number of items on the agendas for these meetings increases each time, and that, since I have noticed that a good number of items don't concern us all, we should work out some sort of criterion for deciding whether an item gets on to the agenda or not.
9	Frank	Criterion? What do you mean?
10	Sheila	Well, how about something like 'an item qualifies for the agenda if it actively involves at least four of us'?
11	Bill	Oh great, just great! I can see we will spend all our time arguing about what 'actively involves' means!
12	Tony	Yes, that would be a difficulty.
13	Frank	I'm not sure this is worth pursuing; we have a heavy agenda ahead.
14	Mike	Suppose we sort out what we mean by 'actively involves' right now?
15	Frank	You started this, Sheila. Have you got a suggestion?
16	Sheila	Have you got a proposal, Mike?
17	Mike	I suggest that an item will actively involve four of us *if*, throughout the time it is discussed, four of us are able and willing to contribute about equally.
18	Bill	That means that items requiring all of us to take action *after* the meeting but that don't necessarily require an involved discussion *during* the meeting won't get on the agenda.
19	Tony	Yes, that's right.
20	Sheila	All right then, have *two* criteria! The first is Mike's one about everyone being involved in the discussion. And the second one can

cope with Bill's point. We could say that an item will 'actively involve' four or more of us if, as a result of the item, we are involved in some form of implementation or action after the meeting.

21 Bill   This is getting more like a law convention every minute!

22 Frank   Please, we are in danger of never getting this meeting started.

23 Mike   Just one more thing before we start. Sheila's idea will help us to whittle down the number of items on the agenda but won't necessarily be a guarantee that we finish meetings on time. So I suggest that we also apportion a certain amount of time to each item which survives the criteria test.

24 Sheila   But you never really know how long you are going to need for an item.

25 Bill   You can say that again. If we had known how long it was going to take to discuss your suggestion . . .

26 Frank   . . . Well, let's get started now.

27 Mike   Hang on. Have we agreed anything or not? Are you suggesting we go ahead and try out these ideas in this current meeting?

28 Tony   I'd be happy to give them a trial run — yes.

29 Sheila   The timetable idea isn't going to work though.

30 Frank   Look, just let me check that I've got all this. The suggestion is that we start our meetings by going down the agenda to check whether each item will involve four or more of us. And that we then agree a time limit for each item?

31 Mike   Yes, and another thought occurs to me. Shall we agree that the author of an item which gets scrapped is responsible for finding alternative ways of dealing with it?

32 Frank   And do we have an agenda prepared beforehand in future? Or shall we each come to

the meeting with items and start by putting them up for the criterion test? Surely that would be best on reflection?

33 Mike   Yes, I think so. Now that we have some criteria to apply, let's kick off future meetings by preparing a communally agreed agenda . . .

34 Sheila I am worried about that. I wasn't thinking of doing away with the advance agenda when I made my suggestion.

35 Bill   I can see that all this will take up more time than it will save.

36 Mike   So let's put an overall time limit on the agenda-setting activities: 15 per cent of the total time for the meeting wouldn't seem excessive.

37 Tony   Yes, I'll go along with that if you agree, Mr Chairman?

38 Frank   It isn't a question of whether or not I agree, it seems.

39 Sheila I suggest we try this now and for the next couple of meetings, and that we then review the procedure to see if it has been successful.

40 Frank   Successful? That's rather a difficult concept to apply to things like meetings.

41 Mike   Well, taking Sheila's idea a bit further, we could agree that success in this context is that we finish this and the next two meetings not more than 10 minutes over time; that we find our contribution rates to be more even . . . and that we can all genuinely rate the meetings to have improved in relevance and usefulness to each of us.

42 Frank   Right! Now let's go ahead and apply this procedure to our current agenda.

What did you conclude about the behaviour of the participants? Did you get a feel for who was most effective and who least effective? If so what criteria did you apply in

making the judgements? I have tried this particular transcript out on a number of people and these are typical
comments: that Tony was just a yes-man: that Bill was
negative and uncooperative: that Frank was a weak, ineffective chairman; that Sheila was very constructive and came
up with the original idea: that Mike was Sheila's main ally
and helped her get her suggestion adopted.

Notice how these 'gut-feel' reactions are drawn from
judgements about two different things. One is the *content*
of what is being said and the other is the *behaviour* used to
express it. To say that Sheila's idea was a good or bad one
is to make a value judgement about the quality of the idea
itself. To debate whether Sheila was persuasive or not is to
comment on the manner in which she put her idea across
to the others. Now, of course, we need to make both sorts of
judgements. The quality of people's contributions is clearly
enormously important. There would be little merit in having
people behaving impeccably if, in doing so, they produced
inadequate ideas. Conversely, it is wasteful to have splendid
ideas that don't get taken up because the behaviour puts
everyone off. We need effective ideas *and* effective behaviour, in parallel, the one facilitating the other.

Notice also how these first-feel reactions plunge into
making value judgements. We quickly decide what is good
and what is bad. We make polarizations between negative
and positive, destructive and constructive, relevant and
irrelevant, effective and ineffective. These are arrived at in
a fairly unthinking way by using our central processor to
label events according to our previously learned attitudes.
To make judgements about other people's behaviour in
this way is fine providing we are not too slap-happy. The
subtleties of human behaviour are such that we are likely
to be wrong at least as often as we are right unless we
become more skilled at monitoring behaviour in more
detail.

One system for deciding who is effective and who ineffective is to apply the in step, out of step criterion we were
practising earlier (Chapter 3). But suppose we want to
enhance this system by going further and pinpointing which
sorts of behaviour are *most appropriate* in securing an objec-

tive? We need some technique for discriminating between different behaviours more precisely than the in step, out of step criterion allows. This is where behaviour categories come in.

BEHAVIOUR CATEGORIES

The actual behaviour categories employed can vary in detail providing they meet the following general criteria:

1 The categories must be relatively simple, mutually exclusive units of behaviour

2 They must be capable of identification by observers with high reliability

3 They must be behavioural or, in other words, must categorize overt behaviour without the need for beneath-the-behavioural-surface interpretations

4 They must be meaningful to the individuals who will use them

5 They must have a relationship with the outcomes of the situations in which they are used

6 Finally, they must refer to behaviour that can change or is capable of modification.

For our immediate purposes I propose to introduce a mere nine categories. They are of course inadequate in giving *complete* coverage. They have been chosen from a list of 50 or so because they cope with the run of the mill verbal behaviours that occur in different transactions. Incidentally, there is also considerable practical merit in only having nine behaviour categories. They are much easier to remember than a longer list. The easier they are to remember the more likely it is that we can use them when monitoring live behaviour and when thinking about which behaviours are most appropriate in different circumstances.

Here are the nine categories together with some guideline definitions:

Seeking ideas   Used whenever someone invites others to contribute ideas, suggestions or proposals. Typical examples are 'Has anyone got any ideas on this one?' 'Chris, have you any suggestions?' and the like.

Proposing   This category is used to cover contributions which contain a possible course of action provided (and this is in contrast to the next category) it is put as a statement, announcement or instruction. Examples are 'I propose that we do so and so', 'We will do the following', "I've got an idea! Let us do so and so', 'I suggest that you do so and so'.

Suggesting   Still used to cover contributions which contain possible courses of action but this time they are expressed as a question. Examples are 'Shall we do so and so?', 'How about doing so and so?', 'Should we do this or that?'

Building   Still basically a contribution that contains a possible course of action and therefore similar to the proposing and suggesting categories. Building is, however, a special kind of proposing or suggesting in that it is used whenever someone adds to, or develops, someone else's idea, suggestion or proposal. Meaningful examples are hard to give out of context but suppose someone put the suggestion: 'Suppose we travel to the meeting together in the same car?' And someone else then said: 'Yes, and if we picked up Ted en route we could prime him for the meeting too'. That would be an example of building. The original course of action has been enhanced by the building behaviour.

Disagreeing   The category used to cover all the various ways in which people disagree. Obvious examples are 'I disagree', 'No, I'm sorry I can't agree with that because . . .'. The category covers flat disagreements as well as those where some reasons or explanation for the disagreement are given.

Supporting Covers all the various ways of agreeing or giving backing to others' contributions. The most obvious ways of doing this are to say things like 'I agree', 'Yes, I support your idea'. More obscure ways of supporting are more verbose, when, for example, someone backs someone else's suggestion by explaining its merits but not actually adding to the suggestion in any way.

Difficulty stating The category used to cover contributions where someone points out the snags, problems and difficulties they see in relation to someone else's contribution. Difficulty stating contributions do not actually contain a disagreement. Classic examples are 'The snag with that would be . . .', 'We wouldn't be able to do that because . . .', 'The problem with that is . . .'. This category is used to cover difficulty stating in relation to the content of what others have said as well as difficulty stating about the context of the interaction. So remarks like 'This is an absolute shambles. We aren't getting anywhere', 'We are running out of time again', 'I can't understand a word you are saying' are all included in this difficulty stating category.

Seeking clarification The category used whenever someone asks for a recap or checks whether he has understood it as it was intended. Examples are 'Do you mean so and so?', 'Just let me check that I've understood what you've said. Your idea is that we do so and so?', 'So you think it would be possible to do so and so?'

Clarifying/explaining/informing This category is used whenever someone provides information ('It is 12 o'clock' 'We have 10,000 stock items') or clarification ('What I meant was . . .') or explanation ('I should explain that the engine requires a mixture of petrol and oil').

Those then are the categories advocated for initial use. As you become used to thinking in terms of these you can add some extra ones to give wider coverage and more precision. In special instances other categories may be required to highlight certain behavioural aspects more. In selling situations, for example, categories such as 'initial greeting', 'benefit statement', 'proof statement', 'overcoming objections', 'close statement' are often employed. In interviewing situations categories such as 'open-ended questions' 'closed questions' are useful. Such changes in emphasis are entirely appropriate and to be expected, provided the behaviour categories used meet the six criteria listed earlier.

Now we are ready to use the categories to describe the behaviour of the participants in the transcript. You might like to turn back to it on pages 83–86 and note down the category into which you feel each contribution falls. Where you notice that the speaker has employed more than one category in his contribution, categorize it by saying to yourself: 'If I were going to speak next, which bit of his behaviour would I react to?' This is simply a way of sorting out which part of his contribution you perceived as the most influential.

Here are my categorizations for the transcript.

1	Frank	Proposing
2	Sheila	Suggesting
3	Frank	Difficulty stating
4	Sheila	Clarifying/explaining/informing
5	Frank	Proposing
6	Tony	Supporting
7	Bill	Difficulty stating
8	Sheila	Proposing
9	Frank	Seeking clarification
10	Sheila	Suggesting
11	Bill	Difficulty stating
12	Tony	Supporting
13	Frank	Difficulty stating
14	Mike	Suggesting
15	Frank	Seeking ideas
16	Sheila	Seeking ideas
17	Mike	Building (on Sheila in 10)
18	Bill	Difficulty stating
19	Tony	Supporting
20	Sheila	Building (on Mike in 17)
21	Bill	Difficulty stating

22	Frank	Difficulty stating
23	Mike	It is not too clear whether this is a fresh proposal or a build on Sheila in 20 and/or 10
24	Sheila	Difficulty stating
25	Bill	He gets cut off prematurely but it is probably difficulty stating
26	Frank	Proposing
27	Mike	Seeking clarification
28	Tony	A vague behaviour, not too clear whether this is informing or supporting
29	Sheila	Difficulty stating
30	Frank	Seeking clarification
31	Mike	Suggesting
32	Frank	Suggesting
33	Mike	Supporting
34	Sheila	Difficulty stating
35	Bill	Difficulty stating
36	Mike	Proposing
37	Tony	Again a vague behaviour. On balance it is probably supporting
38	Frank	Either informing or you may perceive it as difficulty stating but it is a bit obscure
39	Sheila	Proposing
40	Frank	Difficulty stating
41	Mike	Building (on Sheila in 39)
42	Frank	Proposing

How do the categories help? Are they an aid in making 'discoveries' about the importance of certain behaviours that might be missed at a more general descriptive level? Are they an advance on the in step, out of step analysis we tried earlier in the book?

My answers to these questions are an unashamed yes. But let us return to the characters in the transcript and see if I can convince you that the language of the categories helps us to be clearer about the effectiveness of their interaction. Here is my analysis of each participant in turn:

Frank

It looks as though his objective for this part of the discussion was to curtail it and get on with the 'proper' meeting for which they had in fact assembled. Using this as a backcloth his in step, out of step balance sheet looks like this

In step		Out of step	
1	(Proposing)	9	(Seeking clarification)
3	(Difficulty stating)	15	(Seeking ideas)
5	(Proposing)	30	(Seeking clarification)
13	(Difficulty stating)	32	(Suggesting)
22	(Difficulty stating)	38	(Informing or
26	(Proposing)		difficulty stating)
42	(Proposing)	40	(Difficulty stating)
Total	7		6

An uncertain performance, with in step, out of step behaviours practically neck and neck. But now let us use the behaviour categories to scrutinize his in step behaviour more closely to see if they were as appropriate as possible in the light of his objective (or, more correctly, in the light of the objective that we *imagine* has propelled him through the conversation. We are left wondering since he nowhere makes it absolutely explicit). Look at Frank in 3 for example. If his objective was to curtail 'interruptions' and get on with the 'proper' meeting why merely state difficulties? A more appropriate behaviour would have been to disagree. If he had said something like 'No, sorry, Sheila, but I want to press straight on with the agenda items' it is more likely that the issue would have been nipped in the bud and postponed until Any Other Business. It isn't *guaranteed* that this would have worked but it would certainly have increased the probability and that is the best that Frank could be expected to do.

Once Frank had greased his own slippery slope he proceeded to slide down it. In 5, for example, he made a decision that was more in step than out of step with his objective even though it effectively gave Sheila the permission she was seeking to put her proposition now rather than in Any Other Business; 9 was a serious out of step behaviour for Frank. He sought clarification which of course opened the issue up rather than closing it down. What is more, in doing so Frank failed to abide by the decision he announced in 5. A feeble attempt at recovery in 13 with a difficulty state which failed and back to being out of step in 15 again, this time opening up the issue by seeking an idea; 22 is yet another example of a behaviour by Frank aimed at achieving his objective but, as in the earlier examples (3 and 13), it is a difficulty state and not, in the circumstances, nearly potent enough to make it likely that he would succeed.

Frank failed to achieve his objective and deserved to since analysis of his behaviour pinpoints precisely how he lost control. If he had been more conscious of his objective, more skilled at monitoring behaviour and arranging his own so that it was appropriate, the story might have been different.

Sheila

Her objective was rather more transparent than Frank's. We can't be sure of her success standards but broadly her objective must have been to have got her colleagues to adopt her agenda-setting routine in such a way that they would have applied it to the current meeting and agreed to try it at future ones. With this as the backcloth her in step, out of step performance was

In step	Out of step
2 (Suggesting)	24 (Difficulty stating)
4 (Explaining)	29 (Difficulty stating)
8 (Proposing)	34 (Difficulty stating)
10 (Suggesting)	
16 (Seeking ideas)	
20 (Building)	
39 (Proposing)	
Total 7	3

This was a good overall performance that leads to Sheila

being largely successful in achieving her objective; 10, 16 and 20 are particularly skilful contributions: 10 because it would have been so easy to reply to Frank in 9 by giving clarification and, whilst to have done so would still have been in step, it certainly would not have been as potent and appropriate as going ahead with a suggestion: 16 because she explicitly invited Mike to put a suggestion or proposal knowing that it was 'safe' to do so in the light of what Mike had already said in 14: 20 because having brought Mike in she proceeded to build on what he had proposed *and* overcame Bill's difficulty at the same time.

Sheila's behaviour slipped only when she stated difficulties three times about Mike's proposal in 23. In part this was Mike's 'fault' since our analysis left us in doubt about whether Mike was building on Sheila's earlier suggestions or producing an essentially new proposal. If Mike had managed to say 23 in such a way that Sheila had perceived it as building then the difficulties might never have emerged as a reaction. Sheila recovered her behaviour and was entirely back in step by the time she put her proposal in 39.

Bill

It is not too difficult to guess that Bill's objective must have been on the lines of opposing the suggested changes of procedure in such a way that the meeting finishes on time. It is always possible that he had a more obscure objective. You could argue, for example, that he was supporting Sheila's ideas for procedural changes by playing devil's advocate! If so, his colleagues could be forgiven for not realizing it. Alternatively, Bill could have been 'drifting' through this part of the meeting with no objective. If so, it is a shame that he didn't say less. Interactions might often be much more effective if people were built so that they automatically cut-out and their behaviour was frozen whilst they had no conscious, articulatable objective. Rather like the children's game of musical statues: the music stops and you freeze: you can only move again when it restarts. No objective: no behaviour.

If we assume that Bill's objective was to oppose, his in step, out of step performance was

In step		*Out of step*
		7 (Difficulty stating)
		11 (Difficulty stating)
		18 (Difficulty stating)
		21 (Difficulty stating)
		25 (Difficulty stating)
		35 (Difficulty stating)
Total	Nil	6

At least he was consistently out of step! Why was this? At first sight you may have concluded that Bill was opposing fairly effectively? The evidence that he was not is overwhelming.

First, he failed to achieve his objective. Secondly, all his behaviours were out of step with his own objective. Thirdly, the behaviour he employed was singularly inappropriate. Indeed, if you examine the effect that his difficulty statements had on the course of the meeting, the irony is that it succeeded in achieving the reverse of Bill's objective. His difficulty stating actually helped to prolong the meeting and/ or to get Sheila's idea enhanced. Look at the effect of Bill in 18 for example. It led, more or less directly, to Sheila's build in 20. Bill's stated difficulty in 35 had much the same effect, stimulating Mike's proposal in 36. It is true that some of his difficulty statements nearly won useful allies. Bill in 11, for example, was supported by Tony and encouraged Frank to state a difficulty himself in 13. But it was easily counteracted by Mike in 14. Bill seemed to have the same effect on Frank in 21/22 and in 25/26. Bill would have been more likely to succeed if he had either disagreed or put some counter suggestions or proposals. He may have thought he had done his best to oppose but behaviour analysis shows he was using inappropriate behaviours.

Mike

His objective by the time he speaks in 14 seemed to be to have developed Sheila's basic idea in such a way that it became an acceptable, workable proposition. His behaviour was never out of step with this objective.

In step	*Out of step*
14 (Suggesting)	
17 (Building)	
23 (Proposing/Building)?	
27 (Seeking clarification)	
31 (Suggesting)	
33 (Supporting)	
36 (Proposing)	
41 (Building)	
Total 8	Nil

An impeccable performance! He uses in step, entirely appropriate behaviours and achieves his objective. The only slight query is whether in 23 he was producing a new idea or an extension of one of Sheila's. We discussed the effect this confusion seemed to have earlier, when reviewing Sheila's behaviour.

Tony

I suspect he didn't have any objective for the part of the discussion under consideration. Some claim that his objective was to keep everyone happy and be popular. I doubt it, however. He definitely came close to taking sides occasionally and, in any case, if he wanted to achieve this objective he would have had to participate more and use some additional behaviour beyond supporting.

Since Tony had no objective we have no backcloth against which to judge the appropriateness of his behaviour unless we have a try at working out what the communal objective for the discussion was and view his behaviour against that. As we know, there was never any attempt at producing an explicit, group-agreed objective. This is why we have had to use personal or individual objectives exclusively as our backcloth. After the initial skirmish about when Sheila would be allowed to state her idea, the objective of the discussion seems to have been to have decided whether to adopt a change in procedure or not and, if so, to have agreed the details of a workable change.

If we view Tony's behaviour against this objective his five contributions are in step but closer analysis reveals that his behaviour was not as appropriate as it could have been. In fact, it is nearly true to say that if Tony were removed from the transcript nothing that any other participants had to say would need modification. This certainly means that his behaviour failed to make any impact on the behaviour of his colleagues. Accordingly, I conclude that he was coasting through this phase of the meeting with no commitment to any objective.

I hope this analysis has shown how the language of behaviour categories helps in pinpointing which behaviours are appropriate in the light of different objectives. The in step, out of step analysis gives us a general guide which is considerably enhanced by the use of behaviour categories. What the analysis of the transcript cannot demonstrate too well is how we can use the language of behaviour categories to help us interact more effectively in real dynamic interactions. The remaining chapters in this book attempt to show how the benefits of behaviour analysis we described earlier can be achieved on a regular, transaction by transaction basis. Meanwhile, the next chapter gives some more transcripts so that you can have additional practice at categorizing behaviour.

SUMMARY

This chapter has examined what is involved in behaviour analysis. We have seen that fundamentally behaviour analysis is the process of breaking behaviour down into smaller elements than usual so that we can be clearer about the influences of various behaviours. We saw that style-level descriptions such as autocratic, democratic and so on were much too sweeping to give us a clear notion of what was involved in *behaving* the style.

The benefits of behaviour analysis were said to be: that they give a precise language for describing what is going on in an interaction; that they are a practicable means of monitoring our own and other people's behaviour; that the same language 'doubles' as a convenient shorthand when producing a 'behaviour plan' and, finally, that behaviour analysis highlights the shaping effect of certain behaviours on subsequent reactions.

The chapter then went on to concern itself with the first of the four benefits leaving the others to be explored in later chapters. Some introductory behaviour categories were described and applied to the behaviour of some participants in a short transcript. The analysis demonstrated how behaviour categories help to 'firm-up' the in step, out of step analysis so that it is possible to pinpoint precisely which behaviours are most appropriate in the achievement of a particular objective.

6 Exercises in behaviour analysis

This chapter is included to give you, should you wish it, further practice at using the language of the behaviour categories. Having worked through the transcript in the last chapter, and if you feel happy about your ability to use the categories quickly and accurately, you could afford to skip this chapter and move on to Chapter 7 where we see how the categories can be useful in shaping other people's behaviour.

Being able to monitor behaviour unobtrusively in real interactions is dependent on the skill of analysing behaviour using a language or 'labels' of some kind. Whether eventually you choose to use the categories introduced in the last chapter, or to produce some of your own, is immaterial. But the importance of having categories *of some kind* and using them to observe behaviour carefully cannot be overstressed. Unless we can monitor behaviour accurately we cannot reach valid conclusions about it, we cannot work out appropriate behaviours and steer clear of inappropriate ones. Everything emanates from the skill of analysing behaviour.

Clearly the transcripts that follow are inadequate in giving you all the practice you require. In one sense they are easier to analyse because they are less dynamic than a real interaction. You can re-read a contribution, or the whole transcript come to that, as many times as you like in making your analysis. Obviously, real conversations between people do not lend themselves to this sort of double checking. The analysis has to be on an immediate blow-by-blow, behaviour-by-behaviour basis. For this reason, I recommend that if you are going to work through the transcripts that follow you do so by working straight through them fairly swiftly, deciding on the behaviour category immediately after each contribution, rather than reading the whole thing through first. It is better to leave the re-reading for when you check your perceptions with mine.

Perhaps the most serious limitation of written transcripts, making the analysis *more* difficult than with live interactions, is that they only provide information about the actual words that were said. In real life extra aids to speedy analysis are intonation and accompanying non-verbal behaviours such as facial expressions. Try, therefore, to supplement your analysis of the transcripts with some practice at categorizing behaviours during, say, a play on television. Then move on to categorize real conversations as you yourself take part in them. Half the art of categorizing behaviour is to be able to categorize your own contributions as well as those of other people. Transcripts and TV plays will not give you practice at monitoring your own behaviour (unless you are actually in them!) so do not spend too long on them before attempting live interactions.

Three transcripts follow. The first is the sequel to the transcript in Chapter 5 but this time is a conversation between only three of the original characters. Frank, Sheila and Mike. The second is a transcript of three conversations between a personnel manager called Chris and one of his personnel officers called Kathy. Finally, there is a transcript of a meeting at a research and development unit of a large organization. All three transcripts are virtually verbatim accounts of real conversations between real people. I have edited them very little, usually only to make exceptionally long contributions more succinct. I have also changed names of both people and organizations. In each case, my categorizations are given at the end of this chapter on pages 123–130. It would be best if you recorded your categorizations on scrap paper together with a note of the number of the contribution.

First transcript

1	Frank	Now that we've tried out that new procedure for a few meetings let's review how well it's working.
2	Mike	I'm against reviewing it at this stage. It's much too early to review it yet.
3	Frank	Well — I wanted a review because I'm pretty unhappy about the way things are going and I was keen to check your feelings about it before we go any further.
4	Sheila	Okay, How about us doing an *interim* review? There's nothing to be lost surely?
5	Mike	Yes, I suppose that comparing our impressions now, at this stage, with some more meetings to run, could help us to monitor the remaining trials more thoroughly. I suggest we conduct the review with that sort of benefit in mind.
6	Sheila	That's it! Let's agree to conduct this interim review in order to improve the procedure where it already seems to us to be inadequate.
7	Frank	Right! Well, since the new procedure was your idea in the first place, Sheila, I propose you kick this off and tell us how you think it's going.
5	Sheila	I don't agree that it was *my* idea. The final procedure we adopted was more Mike's than mine.
9	Frank	I merely meant that you were the *originator* of the idea.
10	Sheila	I just didn't want Mike's contribution to be overlooked – that's all.
11	Frank	Fair enough — so how about you starting us off then Mike?
12	Mike	I'd like to propose we press on with the procedure pretty well unaltered. I feel it's a vast improvement on anything we've tried previously.

13	Sheila	My own feelings exactly.
14	Mike	I am proposing this because it has certainly been successful in helping us to cut down the number of items on the agenda.
15	Sheila	I couldn't agree more! It has also been successful in making sure that the things we *do* spend time on during the meeting genuinely concern all of us. I agree with Mike; the procedure doesn't need modification at this stage.
16	Mike	That's right! People are certainly more involved.
17	Frank	We aren't going to be able to *improve* the procedure if we just concentrate on its plus points.
18	Mike	What snags have you got in mind then?
19	Frank	Well, I find that as chairman of the meetings there are lots of items which don't get discussed that I *want* to have aired.
20	Sheila	Do you mean that the meetings aren't as useful from your point of view as they were before?
21	Frank	That's right. You see, I used the regular meetings as a convenient way of passing messages and checking up on this and that. In fact, I used to come to the meeting with quite a long checklist of small items and always found that I could dispose of most of them during the meeting.
22	Sheila	Well, while we're talking about snags, the only other one I can think of is time. Putting time limits on each agenda item doesn't seem to work. We have always overrun so far.
23	Mike	Well, any suggestions on how to improve the procedure to overcome these difficulties?
24	Frank	From my point of view I would propose that we scrap it and go back to the way we did things before.
25	Sheila	That's hardly a suggestion for *improvement* Frank.

26	Mike	How about us doing a more thorough 'pros and cons' exercise on this decision?
27	Sheila	Yes, I'd prefer to think this through a bit more carefully before agreeing to scrap it.
28	Frank	Okay. How shall we *do* this?
29	Sheila	I'll collect up the ideas on my pad here. Let's have two columns — one for advantages and one for disadvantages.
30	Mike	Probably better if you do it on the wall board over there, Sheila — then we can all see it as the items go up.
31	Frank	Yes — that'll help us to brainstorm. Suppose we just let our ideas 'rip', and tidy them up afterwards?
32	Sheila	I like it.
33	Frank	I'll tell you what. When we've run out of ideas we can tot them up and see if the disadvantages outweigh the advantages — as I suspect they will. If there are more disadvantages than advantages, I propose we automatically agree to scrap the new procedure.
34	Mike	Sounds as if you're pre-judging the outcome, Frank.
35	Frank	No I'm not! If there *are* more advantages than disadvantages then I'll go along with it quite happily.
36	Mike	Just a minute — remember that it isn't a question of deciding whether to scrap the procedure or not at this stage. Our purpose in producing this list of ideas is so that we can move on to thinking of ways to overcome the disadvantages we identify.
37	Sheila	How about us starting?
38	Mike	Right — let's record the points we have already mentioned like an advantage is that the procedure acts as a filter to cut down the number of items on the agenda.
39	Frank	A disadvantage is that the procedure filters

out items that *I* want dealt with at the meeting.

40	Mike	Another advantage is that the meetings are over quicker.
41	Sheila	You know, I'm finding that I can't get all this down *and* come up with my own ideas.
42	Frank	Well how about us taking it in turns to do the recording then?
43	Sheila	Okay.
44	Mike	I'm not sure that there *is* much more to record. Suppose we work on this disadvantage of Frank's and leave it at that for now?
45	Frank	I'd certainly be happy if we could crack that one.
46	Sheila	What do you mean when you say *work* on this disadvantage?
47	Mike	Simply that we try to produce a modification to the procedure which will overcome the snag Frank is worried about.
48	Sheila	Any ideas then?
49	Frank	Suppose we agreed to have a bit of time set aside for my points as chairman?
50	Mike	Yes, we could end each meeting with a sort of 'chairman's notices' spot. Then everyone would be clear that the agenda setting criteria had been put to one side to give you a special opportunity to raise things which you couldn't otherwise have brought up. Chairman's privilege and all that.
51	Sheila	And how about allocating a time limit for that as we do with the other items of business?
52	Frank	That's great. I think this will overcome my difficulty.
53	Mike	Any ideas on how to introduce this idea to Bill and Tony?
54	Sheila	Well, Bill is sceptical about the benefits of having a procedure at all, so I'm sure he will see this as the first signs that it's crumbling!

		I'd just announce it at the start of the next meeting, Frank.
55	Mike	An alternative would be to tell them the problem and see if they can come up with this proposal themselves.
56	Frank	Hmm. I'd feel that was rather rigged since the three of us have already agreed on it.
57	Sheila	Okay then, I take it that you think it's worth getting Bill and Tony to feel committed; so how about starting off the next meeting by describing the difficulty the procedure gives you, Frank. That's the posing the problem bit. *Then* say that we've thought about it and the only idea we've been able to come up with is this one of having a chairman's notices time as an extra to the normal procedure.
58	Frank	Then bring *them* in by asking if they can think of any other way round the difficulty and deliberately involve them in kicking it around a bit.
59	Mike	And if they come up with something better, we can implement that instead.
60	Frank	Done.

SECOND TRANSCRIPT

Three short linked conversations between Chris, a personnel manager, and Kathy, one of his personnel officers.

1	Chris	I've been feeling that we haven't been communicating as well lately so, let's have a chat about it.
2	Kathy	What do you mean, not communicating well?
3	Chris	Well, you know, you haven't been to see me so much lately.
4	Kathy	When I *do* come, you don't seem very interested in what I have to tell you.
5	Chris	What do you mean by that?

6	Kathy	Well, take last Monday. I was explaining about the recruitment campaign and as soon as Dickie came in with a query you switched off and concentrated on that. I just felt that you weren't really interested in what I had to say: in fact I feel it goes deeper than that. I've noticed that you seem out of touch with what we are doing in the personnel office. It makes me wonder if you really know what is going on.
7	Chris	What makes you think that?
8	Kathy	Well, sometimes you ask me to do something in a hurry and seem to have forgotten that I am already tied up. Just last week you asked me to conduct that impromptu survey among the secretarial staff when you already knew that I was doing the induction course that day.
9	Chris	Okay. A lot of complaints. Shall we take them one at a time and try to agree some actions to prevent them happening again?
10	Kathy	Good idea.
11	Chris	You said that you felt I'm not interested in what you are doing. Any ideas about how that could be overcome?
12	Kathy	Well, a simple action would be for you to resist interruptions when we are having one of our briefing sessions.
13	Chris	Hmm. That's easier said than done. I think it would be unwise to ignore a call from the director, for example.
14	Kathy	I think you have just as much of a responsibility towards your own subordinates as you do to the director. It would do him good to have to wait occasionally anyway. The more you drop everything for him the worse he gets. Look, this is silly. You asked me for a suggestion, I gave you one and now you are pouring cold water on it. Can you suggest a *better* idea?

15	Chris	Sorry. I'm not being very positive am I? Would you accept a slight modification to your idea? Suppose we said that whenever you are in a meeting with me I stop all interruptions except ones from the director himself? He doesn't come through all that frequently after all.
16	Kathy	Okay, and what about adding that our briefing sessions should take place in my office rather than yours? That would make it easier for you to stick to the 'no interruptions' rule as well as giving me and my staff the impression that you were taking an active interest in us.
17	Chris	Yes, we could even plan briefing sessions between us on a regular basis. Every Monday at 10 or something like that.
18	Kathy	I would certainly appreciate that. It would mean that I could save up some items instead of coming through to you all the time with bits and pieces.
19	Chris	Let me summarize what we have agreed then. Every Monday at 10 I am to come to your office for a meeting. I am not allowed to be interrupted except by the director himself.
20	Kathy	Would it also be an idea to give ourselves a time limit for those meetings that we would try to stick to except in unusual circumstances?
21	Chris	Good idea. It means I can schedule the next thing in, knowing that I can make it. What would you think to be an appropriate time limit?
22	Kathy	I suppose an hour.
23	Chris	Fine. That doesn't mean that we have got to pad out our meetings so that they last an hour irrespective does it?
24	Kathy	No, of course not. It just means that neither of us will make any appointments between

10 and 11 on Monday mornings. If our business is over before 11 then that's a bonus.

| 25 | Chris | Shall we agree to try that for the next month and then see if communications between us have improved? |
| 26 | Kathy | Yes. I'm sure they will have. This idea of a regular briefing session will help a lot. |

Next Monday morning

27	Chris	Sorry I'm a bit late, I got caught on the stairs coming down.
28	Kathy	Not a very promising start to our new system.
29	Chris	I've said I'm sorry. Let's get started now I am here. I'll have to be away smartish just before 11.
30	Kathy	But I thought we agreed to hold ourselves free right up till 11?
31	Chris	Oh come on, you're just trying to pick a row. I suggest we get started and that you kick off with the first thing you have got on your list for me.
32	Kathy	No. I'm sorry but I think we should sort this out first. I'm still left feeling that you are here under sufferance and that you aren't really interested in what we are doing down here.
33	Chris	Look, I've said I'm sorry. I don't want to get caught up in a spiral of recriminations. Let's agree to have four of these meetings and then review whether they are adequate after that. Keep a list of the things that bug you if you like, but don't bring them up until the review.
34	Kathy	But storing things up on a list isn't as healthy as saying how you feel as you feel it. But in the circumstances I agree to do it that way for the time being.
35	Chris	Right! I suggest you make a note of that on your list of things that bug you, and then go

ahead and give me the first item you have on today's list.

36 Kathy Well, the first thing is the staffing of the general office. As you know Triss is leaving and Pam obviously will have to go in a couple of months or so. Her baby is due in December.

37 Chris Well, one thing is for sure. You can't replace Triss until after the year end. We are over our establishment on headcount already.

38 Kathy Do you mean the calendar year end or the company one?

39 Chris The company one of course. The calendar year has nothing to do with our headcount figures. I'm saying that you can't replace Triss until the beginning of October.

40 Kathy Have you any suggestions about how we can cope until then?

41 Chris How about getting in temporary help? Temps don't appear on the headcount returns so you could get in as many of those as you liked.

42 Kathy Well, I don't think that temps are any good for our sort of work. I suggest that you do allow us to go ahead and recruit despite the headcount embarrassment.

43 Chris I'm sorry but there is no way that I can agree to that. It's more than my life is worth to be over the top on headcount on the last day of September.

44 Kathy Well, I feel you are being unfair. The only reason you are above establishment is because you took a gamble and brought Joan in, expecting that Susan would have emigrated well before the year end. The difficulty as I see it is that you are making us suffer because of that.

45 Chris Okay then. Would it help if I lent you either Joan or Susan until October when we can start recruiting again?

46	Kathy	It certainly would, and since for some time now you have suspected that the general office wasn't as busy as we have been claiming, Susan could be conducting a survey of the work load whilst she is there.
47	Chris	Okay. I agree to the idea. I'll ask Sue if she would like a spell in the general office.
48	Kathy	How will you put the proposition to her?
49	Chris	Suppose I just ask her if she would mind? Would that do?
50	Kathy	Might it be a better idea for *me* to ask her? That way if she says no I shall only have myself to blame.
51	Chris	Good idea. You sound her out and let me know. Then I'll confirm the arrangement with her.

A month later

52	Chris	Well, we promised ourselves a review. I must say I'm well pleased. Have any improvements to the system occurred to you?
53	Kathy	I don't know whether I've got any *improvements* to suggest. I still find that you seem to be out of touch with our work load when you ask us to take on extra things.
54	Chris	How do you mean, out of touch?
55	Kathy	Well, the other day for example you asked me to get those turnover figures to you pronto and seemed to have forgotten that I was due to interview on the selection panel all that day. Somehow you have the knack of forgetting what other people have told you they are going to be doing.
56	Chris	It's a question of priorities. The director was screaming for those figures and frankly I was surprised that you didn't drop everything to get them to me.
57	Kathy	Well, let me give you another example. Joan was saying that she was surprised you hadn't asked her how her father was. You agreed

to give her a long week-end so that she could go up to Yorkshire to see him in hospital. Then on the Tuesday you rang her and remarked that you hadn't been able to find her on Monday! She says that when she reminded you where she had been you just said 'Oh yes' and left it at that.

| 58 | Chris | You lot do gang up on me don't you? |

59 Kathy But I feel we should be able to discuss this sort of thing openly. How about taking this issue and thinking of some proposals to overcome it then?

60 Chris Yes, all right. Though I can't for the life of me think of an idea that'll get me to remember what's happening to everyone all the time.

61 Kathy Perhaps we don't have to. What say you to the idea of producing a plan for getting you to remember *certain* things about *one* person? The plan could just act as an interim discipline to get you into the swing of remembering.

62 Chris And once I had started to remember as a habit the plan would become redundant you mean?

63 Kathy That's it exactly. Any ideas on what the plan could be?

64 Chris Would tying knots in my handkerchief solve the problem?

65 Kathy It would get a bit bulky in your pocket by the end of the day! What about having an arrangement where I tell you what I'm going to be doing each day and test how well you have remembered at the start of the next day?

66 Chris Yes, that could do the trick. As I got better at remembering we could begin to try me over long periods of time. You know, not daily but weekly eventually. The test could

		take the form of me asking how such and such an activity had gone?
67	Kathy	That sounds great. We'll have you knowing what your personnel officers actually do in no time!
68	Chris	I think we should retain our briefing meetings routine don't you?
69	Kathy	Yes, and I was wondering if the two assistant personnel officers could come along too?
70	Chris	Why not? A good idea. It would make them feel increasingly involved.

THIRD TRANSCRIPT

This is a verbatim account of what was said during a regular monthly meeting in a research and development division. This particular R & D unit is organized as a corporate HQ function offering its expertise to a range of product divisions. A couple of years previously, a rumpus was caused when an internal charging system was introduced and the R & D division was asked to recover at least 50 per cent of its costs in receipts, or revenue, each year. This meant that the R & D division was forced to work harder to 'win' orders from the divisions in the group in competition with external R & D facilities outside the group. The product divisions are free to decide how much to spend on R & D, whether to form their own specialized R & D units or, if not, whether to contract the work inside or outside the group.

In the transcript Dr Roy is a project manager in the R & D division and the meeting is with four of his direct reports. They are Harold, Neil, Alan and Steve. They meet on a regular monthly basis to check on the progress of their various projects.

1	Dr Roy	Does anyone know where Harold is?
2	Neil	He's around. I saw him at lunch time and he has remembered the meeting because he said something about seeing me at two.

3	Dr Roy	Oh well! We'd better start without him. I expect he'll be along in a moment. Let's go through the project list then, checking on progress. Department 'X' is first — that's yours, Alan.
4	Alan	Well, as you know they are very interested in finding materials to replace asbestos. They've had people down to look and I think they are very interested. At the moment they are running some tests themselves to validate the process. If they are successful, the idea is that we would do the remaining bits of development and hand it over to them.
5	Dr Roy	I'm a bit suspicious of these people. Back in December they said they'd make up their minds by the end of January. Now it's May!
6	Alan	I think they are about ready for a discussion to plan what to do next. In fact I'm waiting for them to ring back to say when they want to come.
7	Dr Roy	We're going to get pushed out if we aren't careful. I can't see why they need us, can you?
8	Alan	Well, from our point of view there is certainly less in it if they decide to use their own R & D facilities. But I feel they won't want to offend us.
9	Dr Roy	Shouldn't we be showing why they need to spend £5500 or £10 000 with us?
10	Alan	Well, I think they *must* be interested to have come and looked in the first place.
11	Dr Roy	I see. So they are supposed to be coming to talk it over?
12	Alan	That's right. Until then we are as uncertain as everyone else.
13	Dr Roy	We'll just have to wait and see. This next one is yours, too, Alan. Tell us about progress.

14	Alan	Yes, well, some samples have been sent. I contacted them a month or so ago and they said they were still thinking about it.
15	Dr Roy	You told us that last time. What, if anything, has happened since? Wasn't Bert supposed to have asked them when he went to the other meeting a couple of weeks back?
16	Alan	Yes, I'm not sure whether he did though.
17	Dr Roy	I think so. I'm sure I saw a copy of a letter. I forget the context just now.
18	Alan	Oh. Well, he must have then.
19	Dr Roy	You'd better check up on that one. They are probably playing for time. Or are we? Don't answer that! Right! What about the Permatract proposal, Neil?
20	Neil	Well, as you know, they accepted the feasibility study and that was followed up with a proposal worth about £10 000. They say the cash can't be raised this year and that they hope to fit it into next year's budget.
21	Dr Roy	Oh dear! Did you actually go and talk to them about it?
22	Neil	Well, no, it was done on the 'phone.
23	Dr Roy	So you've been spared that one now. And we have been spared £10 000 as well it seems. Shall we lose it for a bit then?
24	Nel	Yes, and resurrect it when things are better.
25	Dr Roy	Right. This is all very depressing. What about your project, Steve?
26	Steve	Technically there is no doubt we'll get there, as you know. The tests are going very well indeed. The problem is going to be the exploitation. We'll have a product and a mythical market.
27	Dr Roy	Yes, but that's their problem isn't it? We aren't open to any criticism.
28	Steve	Yes, I suppose so. I think I may be being unduly pessimistic. An encouraging sign is

		that next time they are bringing a marketing consultant with them!
29	Dr Roy	I don't know whether that's a good sign or a bad sign. By the way, Steve, what happened about the mysterious coating techniques report? Did it ever turn up?
30	Steve	I'm sure that's really irrelevant in this meeting — but no, I'm still chasing it.
31	Dr Roy	I think I'd better have a word with Geoff and see what's happening.
32	Steve	So am I supposed to be chasing that, or you? We'd better be careful we aren't adding tᵣ the confusion on that one!
33	Dr Roy	You'd better leave it to me. As soon as I get it I'll let you have a copy naturally.
34	Steve	All right then. I'd have thought it better if I did it but still if you'd rather, it's one less thing for me to do!

Enter Harold

35	Harold	Sorry I'm late. Got stuck talking about the ventilators in the second lab.
36	Dr Roy	What did they have to say about them, as a matter of interest?
37	Harold	Oh! They're all faulty as I've always said. The whole lot have got to come out and start all over again.
38	Dr Roy	Oh Lord! Wish I hadn't asked you now! How long will it take?
39	Harold	Well, they *say* a couple of weeks. But I don't believe it! It *ought* to take half that time. But I bet it takes double: four weeks or more I'd say!
40	Dr Roy	Well, I'm sure we can count on you to keep an eye on them and generally chivy them along. Now where were we? Oh yes, department Y. Back to you, Neil.
41	Neil	Last time I spoke to them they said to chase them again in the autumn.
42	Dr Roy	Okay. Well here's our new little shining

light — gas burners. That wasn't supposed to be a joke, but thank you for laughing all the same! Now this one is *really* hopeful. The empirical tests on the new pipes look good. We took one of the proto-types and played a gas flame on it. Then blew cold air down it and you'd hardly know it had been touched. It was very impressive. Anyway they now want a quote for us to make up a longer piece of pipe. About 36 in. If we can pull this off it could be really big. There are about 200 pipes in each boiler you see. All we've got to do is make the little blighters and we're there I reckon.

43	Steve	What about creep? How do they show up under test?
44	Dr Roy	Well, *they* are doing creep tests. But it's all pretty useless because they won't creep. Still it gives them something to do.
45	Harold	I'd like to talk about this manhole cover thing.
46	Dr Roy	Right. Fire away!
47	Harold	I've had a couple of preliminary conversations with them. At present they use the normal 18 in × 24 in cast iron cover. Or rather, it's a cast iron basket really, filled with 3 in or 4 in of low grade concrete. The problem seems to be that they have to send out more men than are needed for inspection work simply because they are needed to lift the manhole covers! They are asking if we can make manhole covers that are as durable, but light enough for one man to lift.
48	Steve	Do you mean they literally wish us to *make* them? Or to do all the R & D involved in coming up with a new design?
49	Harold	Well, we couldn't make them could we! We aren't in the production business.

50	Steve	But do we *want* to do this? Do we want to embark on a development programme to construct and test an alternative cover?
51	Dr Roy	Why not? If there's money in it. How much do the current covers cost to make, Harold?
52	Harold	The economics aren't straightforward. It isn't just a question of production costs. As I've explained, the present covers cost them *indirectly* in increased labour overheads. One man can't lift the present cover on his own you see. Or so the unions claim anyway! But they would wouldn't they! It's back to 'jobs for the boys again' basically!
53	Neil	Have you done any testing on the current covers, Harold?
54	Harold	Well, we've broken a few using a 6 in steel pad to simulate the tyre of a lorry. The funny thing is that the concrete doesn't seem to make any difference to the strength.
55	Neil	Where *do* they break, in fact?
56	Dr Roy	And under what conditions? Centrally loaded with the covers fully or partially supported?
57	Harold	Look! They aren't going to be impressed with academic stuff! I can tell them enough about how the current ones break — rest assured!
58	Neil	If the concrete doesn't make any contribution why don't they leave it out and turn them upside down? That would make them lighter.
59	Harold	Ah! I've misled you there. The iron basket doesn't have a bottom to it. The sides are slightly wedge shaped, you see, and that stops the concrete falling through.
60	Dr Roy	It's a St George's cross is it Harold?
61	Harold	Yes, in cast iron as I've explained.
62	Dr Roy	A St Andrew's cross would be stronger. I

wonder why they don't use a St Andrew's cross?

63	Harold	Because the present construction is *strong* enough! They want something equally strong but lighter.
64	Steve	Well I'd like to be clearer about the criteria we need to use to decide whether to get involved in something like this.
65	Dr Roy	Suppose we kept the cast iron basket and found a replacement for the concrete filler?
66	Neil	I think that if they just want us to replace concrete with a lighter fill, it's not a technical job for us.
67	Harold	Not technical? What do you mean? I'll remind you that de-technical is an emotive term around here, with respect, I must disagree totally with you. At least this work could mean we do something really practical and useful for once!
68	Dr Roy	Hmm. Must admit I'm still wondering if there is a credible alternative to concrete.
69	Neil	Some kind of plastic dish perhaps?
70	Alan	Marine ply?
71	Dr Roy	Yes, a sheet moulded compound. What sort of density material could we offer as an alternative to the concrete?
72	Neil	I'd say 2 as opposed to about 2.5 for low grade concrete.
73	Dr Roy	Is that all?
74	Neil	I think you ought to find out if they would accept the same breaking load as now; what the current covers cost to make; what it will save to have a lighter one and so on. When we know all this we can sit down and do some unsophisticated calculations.
75	Dr Roy	If we are talking about 2 as opposed to 2.5 it is certainly a question of redesigning the whole thing, not just replacing the filler with something lighter, that's for sure.
76	Harold	Anyway. None of this is helping me much!

		I'm meeting them early next week. What should I say? Are we interested or not?
77	Dr Roy	I should play it by ear for the time being, Harold. You can get an idea of how they are feeling, their enthusiasm, the funding situation and so on.
78	Harold	What cost shall I quote then?
79	Dr Roy	You need to break it down into the usual steps. That's why I suggest you play it by ear. You'll soon know whether to put in a bid for a simple feasibility study or whether to mention a bigger package that includes a feasibility study as a first stage only.
80	Harold	Okay. I wish the meeting had been a little more *certain* about this. It all seems so vague.
81	Steve	I'm inclined to agree. I've been sitting back listening to all this, and I really think we ought to spend some time in one of these meetings planning our revenue strategy as a group. I feel that if we five were clearer about our objectives, the criteria we should use to decide whether to go for something or not, and so on, we'd get on far better. As a newcomer I feel these meetings are very unproductive.
82	Dr Roy	All meetings are unproductive. The real work is what happens in between meetings. This meeting is just supposed to be a monthly check on progress with our revenue earning projects. Nothing more. It's simply a question of working down this list and updating the 'comments' column. And that's exactly what we've just done, isn't it?
83	Steve	No, not really. This thing about the manhole covers hasn't been like that. I felt that Harold wanted some help from us — wanted some decisions. He wasn't merely reporting on progress.

84	Dr Roy	Then Harold was clearly out of order. He shouldn't have brought it up here.
85	Harold	With respect, Mr Chairman, in that case *you* were out of order in allowing the matter to proceed! What is said and not said at a meeting is entirely a function of the chairman.
86⁻	Dr Roy	Oh, I can't accept that! We are all adults. Surely, I'm not supposed to be cracking a big whip around here? That's not my style. I want to operate informally.
87	Steve	Well, I think it's all right to operate informally providing it's not at the cost of communication confusion, frustration of group members and so on.
88	Neil	It seems fair enough, Roy. How about setting some time aside to kick all this around and come up with an agreed *modus operandi?* It couldn't do any harm and it might clear the air a bit.
89	Dr Roy	Very well, if that's what you want. How about you, Alan? You've been very quiet?
90	Alan	I'm quite happy with things as they are but I'll go along with the majority on this.
91	Dr Roy	Right! Well that's settled. We've made a decision! Are you happier, Harold?
92	Harold	Not really. I don't want to sit around deciding how to reach decisions. I just want to get on and do it!
93	Dr Roy	Well, we'll discuss that next time shall we? Now, anyone got anything else? . . . No? Well, I know it isn't strictly relevant to this meeting but, particularly in view of our discussion just now, I thought you might like to know what we discussed about the corporate plan at the last divisional meeting. The divisional head circulated a paper — I've got it here somewhere, I think; Oh well, never mind, I can remember the main points. The idea is to

have a strategy that can pull all the bits and pieces we do as a division together. Give them some cohesion. The divisional head thinks we should be better at dropping programmes that aren't in the main stream too. He thinks people follow their own inclinations too much without enough consideration of the revenue implications.

94	Steve	I'm glad you're telling us this Roy. It's exactly what I was on about earlier — except that it's on a bigger scale. But the considerations are the same. The need for an agreed strategy to underpin all we're doing and so on.
95	Dr Roy	The only other point is that the divisional head wants us to move away from getting receipts by doing rubbish. He maintains that it isn't good for staff morale just to do odd jobbing to gain credibility.
96	Harold	I've been saying that for years! They ought to lay down firm guidelines.
97	Dr Roy	Let's leave it there, shall we? We can take all this up again in our next meeting.
98	Steve	When will that be, Roy?
99	Dr Roy	Well, a month from now brings us to . . .
100	Neil	Can it wait that long? Shouldn't we sneak one in earlier since we've identified so many basic issues that need sorting out?
101	Dr Roy	Oh! I'd have thought a month will give us time to meditate.
102	Steve	How about next Wednesday? I agree with Neil I don't think it can wait really.
103	Dr Roy	Next Wednesday is no good for me. I'll be up talking to department W on that day.
104	Harold	What about? Have you mentioned that before? Where is it on the list?
105	Dr Roy	Whoops! Sorry, I've obviously put my foot in it again. It's a very preliminary enquiry from them at this stage so I was going to

bring it up if and when things became a little more certain.

106 Harold But things don't have to be a dead cert before they go on our list, do they? I thought the idea was to list *all* our revenue earning projects. Not just those we choose to!

107 Neil Let's not take that up for now, but it does underline, yet again, the need for us to have a basic sort out, Roy.

108 Steve Is next Thursday any good?

109 Dr Roy Yes, if it were in the afternoon. How about everyone else? Next Thursday at 2 o'clock say? Okay? Going, going, gone! Golly! You know what we've done? Agreed to have a meeting about a meeting. I hope it's worth it!

110 Harold So do we!

BEHAVIOUR CATEGORIES FOR FIRST TRANSCRIPT

1 Proposing
2 Disagreeing
3 Explaining
4 Suggesting
5 Building (on 1 and 4)
6 Building (on 5)
7 Proposing
8 Disagreeing
9 Explaining
10 Explaining
11 Suggesting
12 Proposing
13 Supporting
14 Explaining
15 Supporting
16 Supporting
17 Difficulty stating

18 Seeking information
19 Informing
20 Seeking clarification
21 Clarifying
22 Informing
23 Seeking ideas
24 Proposing
25 Difficulty stating
26 Suggesting
27 Supporting
28 Seeking ideas
29 Proposing
30 Building (on 29)
31 Building (on 29 and 30)
32 Supporting
33 Proposing (possibly building on 29)
34 Difficulty stating
35 Disagreeing
36 Clarifying
37 Suggesting
38 Informing
39 Informing
40 Informing
41 Difficulty stating
42 Suggesting (possibly building on 29/30 but in real life, unless it was specifically flagged, it is unlikely you could link it back that far)
43 Supporting
44 Suggesting
45 Supporting
46 Seeking clarification
47 Clarifying
48 Seeking ideas
49 Suggesting
50 Building (on 49)
51 Building (on 49 and 50)
52 Supporting
53 Seeking
54 Proposing
55 Proposing

56 Difficulty stating
57 Building (on 55)
58 Building (on 57)
59 Building (on 58)
60 Supporting

BEHAVIOUR CATEGORIES FOR SECOND TRANSCRIPT

1   Proposing
2   Seeking clarification
3   Clarifying
4   Difficulty stating
5   Seeking clarification
6   Informing
7   Seeking clarification
8   Informing
9   Suggesting
10 Supporting
11 Seeking ideas
12 Proposing
13 Difficulty stating
14 Seeking ideas
15 Building (on 12)
16 Building (on 15)
17 Building (on 16)
18 Supporting
19 Summarizing
20 Building (on 17)
21 Seeking ideas
22 Proposing
23 Seeking clarification
24 Clarifying
25 Suggesting
26 Supporting
27 Explaining
28 Difficulty stating
29 Proposing
30 Difficulty stating

31 Proposing
32 Disagreeing
33 Proposing
34 Supporting (under duress!!)
35 Proposing
36 Informing
37 Difficulty stating
38 Seeking clarification
39 Clarifying
40 Seeking ideas
41 Suggesting
42 Proposing
43 Disagreeing
44 Difficulty stating
45 Suggesting
46 Building
47 Supporting
48 Seeking ideas
49 Suggesting
50 Building
51 Supporting
52 Seeking ideas
53 Difficulty stating
54 Seeking clarification
55 Informing
56 Explaining
57 Informing
58 Difficulty stating
59 Suggesting
60 Difficulty stating
61 Suggesting
62 Seeking clarification
63 Seeking ideas
64 Suggesting
65 Suggesting
66 Building (on 65)
67 Supporting
68 Suggesting
69 Building (on 68)
70 Supporting

BEHAVIOUR CATEGORIES FOR THIRD TRANSCRIPT

1 Seeking information
2 Informing
3 Proposing
4 Informing
5 Difficulty stating
6 Informing
7 Difficulty stating
8 Informing
9 Suggesting
10 Informing
11 Seeking clarification
12 Clarifying
13 Proposing
14 Informing
15 Seeking clarification
16 Clarifying
17 Informing
18 Informing (but it is vague)
19 Seeking information
20 Informing
21 Seeking information
22 Informing
23 Suggesting
24 Supporting
25 Seeking information
26 Difficulty stating
27 Suggesting
28 Informing
29 Seeking information
30 Informing
31 Proposing
32 Seeking clarification
33 Clarifying
34 Supporting (under duress!)
35 Explaining
36 Seeking information
37 Informing

38 Seeking information
39 Informing
40 Proposing
41 Informing
42 Informing
43 Seeking information
44 Informing
45 Proposing (by the skin of its teeth. Very vague!)
46 Supporting
47 Informing
48 Seeking clarification
49 Clarifying
50 Seeking clarification
51 Seeking clarification
52 Informing
53 Seeking information
54 Informing
55 Seeking information
56 Seeking information
57 Informing
58 Suggesting
59 Clarifying
60 Seeking information
61 Informing
62 Seeking clarification
63 Explaining
64 Informing (not explicit enough to be a proposal)
65 Suggesting
66 Proposing
67 Disagreeing
68 Informing
69 Suggesting
70 Suggesting
71 Seeking information
72 Informing
73 Seeking clarification
74 Proposing
75 Explaining
76 Seeking suggestions
77 Proposing

78 Seeking ideas
79 Explaining
80 Difficulty stating
81 Proposing (but it is very vague. You could be
    forgiven for thinking it was difficulty stating)
82 Explaining
83 Disagreeing
84 Difficulty stating
85 Disagreeing
86 Disagreeing
87 Informing
88 Suggesting
89 Seeking information
90 Supporting (?)
91 Seeking information
92 Difficulty stating
93 Informing
94 Supporting
95 Informing
96 Supporting
97 Suggesting
98 Seeking information
99 Proposing
100 Suggesting
101 Explaining
102 Building (on 100)
103 Difficulty stating
104 Seeking clarification
105 Explaining
106 Difficulty stating
107 Proposing
108 Suggesting
109 Suggesting (or difficulty stating?)
110 Supporting

Note on the categorizations for the third transcript

If you have worked through the third transcript, it will not
have escaped your notice that there is a lot of clarifying,
explaining and informing. In fact it works out at about 70

per cent of the total. In my experience this is a suspiciously high level in meetings other than pure briefing or information-exchanging ones. Of course, there will always be a need for important behaviours like giving clarifications, seeking and giving information and so on but, if a discussion indulges itself in these sorts of behaviours to the exclusion of others, it is unlikely to finish up having agreed on anything. The discussion will, in effect, have been starved of those behaviours that are required in thrashing out a sound course of action to which participants can subscribe. If this is to happen, there must be suggestions and proposals and reactions to them (be they building and supporting or disagreeing and difficulty stating). I have found that when participants in a meeting *feel* that it is going round in circles and not really getting anywhere, that correlates with a disproportionate amount of information giving. Dr Roy is a past master at retreating into information just when one of the other categories would have been more productive. The best examples of this are in the first phase of the meeting, up to 44, where time and time again things are left in the air with no actions agreed. Good examples are 13, 19, 29; 23 is nearly another example because whilst it contains a suggested course of action 'shall we lose it for a bit then?', it is hardly a scintillating one in the context of the conversation.

My conclusion on clarifying, explaining and informing is that they are necessary; that they will frequently account for a high percentage of what goes on in an interaction (one reason for this is the obvious one that it is not one category but three and will inevitably occur more frequently therefore); and finally that, depending on the objectives of the occasion, if they exceed, say, 50 per cent of the total of all behaviours it signals the danger of action deprivation. The next chapter, on behaviour shaping, will help you to understand why this should be so.

SUMMARY

In this chapter we have looked at three transcripts of interactions with the object of practising the skill of monitoring behaviour using the language of the behaviour categories. I have argued that this is a fundamental skill, since there would be little point in troubling to arrange our behaviour in certain ways if we were unable to monitor the effects of having done so. Giving more conscious thought to our behaviour in relation to objectives inevitably involves the skill of monitoring our own as well as other people's behaviour unobtrusively and accurately.

7 How to shape other people's behaviour

The way we behave is not a matter of any concern unless it is true that our behaviour significantly affects the behaviour of those with whom we interact. All behavioural scientists make the assumption that there *is* a link between one person's behaviour and another's.

In the first chapter of this book I tried to establish by examples that, since our behaviour is by definition always directly observable, it makes a direct impact on the behaviour of others. Since then, at intervals throughout the book, I have promised that we shall return to this crucial process and examine it in more depth.

If you fundamentally object to the notion that in many situations the prime object of behaving at all is to influence others, then behaviour shaping is not for you! Before you reject it out of hand, however, I shall reiterate that I disagree with using behaviour to manipulate people into positions of acceptance. In part I object on ethical grounds and, even leaving that aside, I object because it is patently inefficient. Sooner or later people know they have been manipulated and the resultant cost in resentment, lack of trust and subsequent suspicion is too high a price to pay. It more than negates any short-term gain.

Behaviour shaping is not therefore some sort of gimmick or an easy ploy to ensure one-upmanship. It is simply a natural extension of the points we have already explored: the easy visibility of behaviour; the need to arrange our behaviour so that it is appropriate to the objectives of the occasion; the need to monitor our behaviour in relation to the reactions and behaviour of others.

The word 'shaping' in this context is used to describe the process of arranging your own behaviour so that it influences (shapes) the behaviour returned to you by another person. This process is going on throughout any interaction whether you are consciously aware of it or not. The gain in making a 'natural' process a *conscious* one is that we can harness the behaviour shaping processes more efficiently. Someone who has learned how to arrange his or her own behaviour so that it shapes that of others to mutual advantage is more likely to achieve his or her objectives than someone who has not.

Behaviour shaping is, however, by no means a selfish one-sided affair. The likelihood of helping other, perhaps less skilled, people to achieve their objectives and of achieving mutually advantageous outcomes is also greatly increased.

In the first chapter I gave some simple examples of behaviour shaping at work. Most of them were non-verbal like yawning, smiling and head nodding. An obvious *verbal* example of the behaviour shaping process is found in the relationship between questions and answers. You ask a question and the usual effect is that it will stimulate an answer as a response. If you ask an open-ended question it will be more likely to 'shape' a longer-winded answer than if you ask a closed one, and so on. An example of an open-ended question is 'How are things going in your new job?' A closed question is 'Got a new job haven't you?' The shaping effect of a question is, not always but usually, to provoke an answer. What then of the behaviour categories introduced in Chapter 5? What are their behaviour shaping roles?

Over the years I have researched the 'cause and effect' links between the different categories on our list by analysing the sequential patterns in interactions. This is done by a blow by blow analysis of the behaviour categories using abbreviations so that the categories can be captured in the sequence in which they actually occured. A typical analysis would therefore look like the following.

SI   (Seeking ideas)
P   (Proposing)
DS   (Difficulty stating)
E   (Explaining)
B   (Building)

After analysing a few hundred interactions of various kinds I do a count to discover which behaviour follows which most frequently. From these findings I begin to build up a picture of the behaviours that are instrumental in evoking certain responses.

The assumption is that behaviour breeds behaviour or, in other words, that each behaviour acts as a stimulus triggering a response which, in turn, becomes the stimulus for the next response and so on in a chronological chain reaction.

Information about how behaviours actually function and the effects they have on people's reactions, is enormously helpful in deciding which behaviours to use and which to avoid in order to achieve a given objective. The way people react to our behaviour is crucial to our success. This is why I have emphasized the importance of including behavioural standards as part of the end of interaction objective. If you look back at some of the illustrations of objectives in earlier chapters you will see how often a substantial element is concerned with whether or not we, through our behaviour, brought about certain observable reactions in others. Often they are spontaneous utterances about the usefulness of the interaction from their point of view. You may object that people do not say what they mean frequently enough to make these a significant guide to success. But remember that we only have access to their overt behaviour and must use it as best we can as an indirect 'window' on what they really think or feel beneath the behavioural surface.

'Actions speak louder than words', it is often claimed, but in interactions words are frequently the closest we can hope to get to actions. In any case, if we can influence people impressively enough during an interaction we stand a good chance of closing the gap between actions and words. If people leave an interaction deeply committed to doing something, so deeply committed that they *say so* as they leave, they are more likely to do it than if they leave unimpressed and saying they will do something as a means of securing their early exit. If only we could shape behaviour more effectively, cynical comments such as 'When all is said and done, far more is said than done' need never have any bite again. Let us go through each of the behaviour categories pinpointing their behaviour shaping effects. Most of my research findings should accord with your own experiences, because I am only quoting from the sequential monitoring done whilst observing real, on the job, interactions. I have been careful to keep separate the stockpile of observations from 'artificial' interactions that took part on training programmes. This is because interactions on contrived behaviour change programmes are not necessarily representative of what happens in interactions in the normal work place.

THE BEHAVIOUR SHAPING EFFECTS OF THE BEHAVIOUR CATEGORIES INTRODUCED IN CHAPTER 5

Let us look at precisely how each of the behaviour categories introduced earlier function. The statistics are simple; a percentage is given which indicates how many times out of a hundred a particular behavioural reaction occurred. The strongest trends are those that occurred on 20 per cent or more of occasions. The 'also rans' which were found to occur on between 10 per cent and 19 per cent of occasions are also shown. Any reactions which occurred on less than 10 per cent of occasions are not shown because, with this low level of probability, the trend is not strong enough to be reliable.

Seeking Ideas Asking other people for their ideas

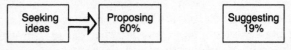

The most likely reaction to this behaviour is, as you might

expect, a proposal or suggestion. Statistically a proposal is more likely than a suggestion simply because proposals, in the strict sense in which we differentiate between them and suggestions, (see Chapter 5, page 89) occur at least twice as often as suggestions.

Behaviour which seeks ideas is therefore a powerful shaping behaviour since it is relatively easy to predict its effects accurately. The data show that eight times out of ten an idea is forthcoming. Even so, this cannot be *guaranteed*. We are merely observing that it is statistically highly probable that a proposal or suggestion will occur in the wake of this behaviour. If, for example, the person with whom you are interacting has no ideas, you can continue to seek ideas to no avail. Behavioural skills do not compensate for ignorance!

Proposing Putting forward ideas (possible courses of action) as statements

There are two likely reactions to proposals. The most likely, alas, is a difficulty statement, which occurs on four out of ten occasions. The next most likely is a supporting statement which happens on a quarter of occasions. If people are not ready to react in one of these two ways, they will most probably ask questions about the proposal which explains why 'seeking clarification' is an 'also ran' at 16 per cent.

Suggesting Putting forward ideas as questions.
(for example 'How about doing so and so?')

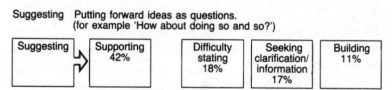

The fascinating distinction between suggesting and proposing statements is that suggestions cause supporting to edge ahead of difficulty stating as a reaction. In other words, if you put an idea forward as a proposal you run a greater

risk of running into difficulties than if you put the very same idea as a suggestion. Furthermore, even if your idea is inadequate, expressing it as a suggestion makes it more likely that people will build on it.

So suggesting is an important alternative to proposing when you are in a situation where your objective puts a premium on securing agreement. Again I should warn that behaviour shaping is not magic; suggestions are still met with difficulty statements and disagreement! We are talking about arranging our behaviour to make it as likely as possible that it has the desired effect on other people. Even if we fail we shall do so having done all we could to succeed; and that is the best that anyone can do.

A statement seeking clarification is also quite possible in the wake of a suggestion just as it was after a proposal.

Building   Developing someone else's idea:

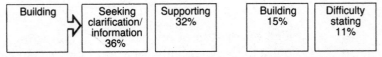

People react in one of two ways after a piece of building behaviour. If they are clear that it *was* building behaviour they support it. If they are not clear *what* it was they seek clarification. This difference is totally dependent on the perception of the person on the receiving end of the building statement. Building is one of those behaviours which is likely to be misunderstood. By contrast, behaviours like supporting and disagreeing leave people in little doubt. Building behaviour, on the other hand, often leaves people confused and in need of clarification.

This raises an important proviso that applies to all the behaviour-shaping data. To put it at its simplest, people are not going to react to our behaviour in the ways the data predict unless they perceive the behaviour in the way we intend. For example, it is no use *imagining* you are employing building behaviour and leaving those with whom you are interacting in the dark. They may well fail to link your building behaviour to an earlier suggestion or proposal, in which case the chances are they will react to it as an *alternative* proposal or suggestion. This is particularly hazardous and, should this happen, the likelihood of this producing disagreement or a difficulty statement is high.

To some extent this proviso applies to all our behaviour. Clearly, if people aren't clear what we are up to behaviourally, the risks that they will interpret it 'wrongly' (in our perception) are much greater. The solution is to 'flag' your behaviour frequently and certainly to be careful to 'flag' building statements since they are extra risky. By 'flagging' I literally mean including a behavioural commentary in your contribution. This does not mean using the 'jargon' of the category labels (unless you are lucky enough to be inter-acting with someone who uses them also, in which case they won't be jargon: jargon is in the eye of the beholder), nor need it be laborious. Here are some examples of 'flagging' using everyday parlance:

'This is an idea off the top of my head . . .' (suggesting)
'I'd like to put up an Aunty Sally for you to kick around' (suggesting)
'I propose that . . .' (proposing)
'I've just been thinking about Bill's earlier idea that we . . . I'd like to add to it by suggesting . . .' (building)
'I like that idea! Can I develop it further by proposing . . .' (building)
'I'd like to say something in support of that' (supporting)
'I'd like to play devil's advocate with that idea for a few minutes' (difficulty stating)
'I'm going to disagree with that and explain why' (disagreeing)
'Could I just check that I have got this straight? As I understand it you are suggesting that . . .' (seeking clarification)

This is not an exhaustive list. You may realize that you have some characteristic phrases that you use to give this sort of behavioural guide to people. What is fatal is to flag a piece of behaviour incorrectly. People will often say

'I'd like to develop that idea a bit . . .' and then go on to put up an alternative that isn't a development at all.

My conclusion is that flagging, providing it is correct, is enormously helpful in a conversation because it helps to shape people's perception of behaviour and in consequence their reactions. I have noticed that the tendency to give an explicit behavioural pointer correlates with other interactive skills and successes. I am satisfied that flagging is one of the outward signs of interactive competence. (See Chapter 10).

To return to building behaviour specifically, *if* it is recognized as building behaviour the likelihood of support is very high. The other fascinating thing is that a building statement, as a *reaction* to a building statement, occurs more frequently than at any other time. It seems that a building statement begets a building statement and there can be quite a chain of them often in short, excited bursts. Many brainstorming techniques recognize this and try to create behavioural conditions where creativity (behaviourally, that is to say, producing lots of 'good' suggestions, proposals and building statements) can flourish. It is particularly interesting that so many brainstorming techniques explicitly forbid reactions of the difficulty stating and disagreeing kind. This is an example of a behaviour plan and we shall turn our attention to such matters in Chapter 9.

Disagreeing   Explicitly disagreeing with something someone else has said

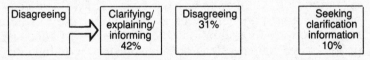

Disagreement provokes two strong reactions. Either people react 'defensively' and assume that the disagreement has sprung from a misunderstanding. In this case they naturally try clarifying, explaining or informing. On the other hand people can react 'aggressively' and simply disagree back! Since aggression breeds aggression this can develop into a disagreeing spiral. I have watched people get sucked into the disagree-disagree spiral many times. It is particularly prevalent in management and trade union negotiations and on the domestic front, between husband and wife. This is not to condemn disagreement. It can be a useful way to sort things out. Indeed, in our culture, there are signs that we put high value on disagreeing as a behaviour. Most debating procedures, be they in the Oxford Union, Parliament or on television, are deliberately structured to promote disagreement. This serves to remind us that whether disagreeing behaviour is appropriate or not depends on circumstances and objectives. Sometimes it is a stimulating behaviour that paves the way to getting people to change their minds about something. Sometimes it is a pointless, destructive behaviour that ends up in an entrenched slanging match that nobody wins.

Supporting   Agreeing with something someone else has said

Supporting behaviour seems to act as a behavioural fertilizer. It either encourages more suggestions/proposals or, much more likely, it has the effect of so heartening the person being supported that he says his idea all over again! Support is therefore most frequently followed by an often lengthy piece of clarification. This is likely to be the response even if repetition of the idea is superfluous. So verbal support acts in much the same way as non-verbal support such as head nodding and other signals of approval; all push up reiteration whether they have been explicitly called for or not. Supporting behaviour is particularly useful, therefore, if you are in a situation where you want to encourage people to participate. It is not an appropriate behaviour if you are trying to curtail someone who is verbose!

Difficulty stating   Pointing out the snags or difficulties with something someone else has said

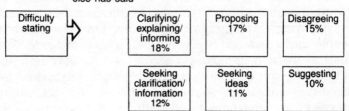

Difficulty stating is a fascinating behaviour which is widespread but totally uncertain in its behaviour shaping effects. I have observed literally thousands of difficulty stating behaviours and still no clear response pattern emerges. The following responses, however, are the most likely:

Clarifying, explaining, informing
The response of clarifying, explaining or informing occurs, just as it does after disagreement, when people assume that the difficulty statement has resulted from a misunderstanding.

Proposing
A proposition is a likely response when people take up the challenge that a difficulty statement poses. This particularly applies when the difficulty stating is done in a 'let me play devil's advocate' way.

Disagreement
Disagreement occurs when people think the difficulty statement is unwarranted and/or when they mistake the difficulty statement for disagreement. It seems that people often 'read between the lines' of a difficulty statement and make the implied disagreement an explicit one.

There are other reactions in the wake of difficulty statements such as seeking clarification, seeking ideas and suggestions but the likelihood of them occurring is progressively less strong.

My conclusion from this selection of likely responses is that difficulty stating behaviour is unreliable in the sense that its effects are so unpredictable. Difficulty stating behaviour is a good example, therefore, of a behaviour that needs to be flagged explicitly, so that it is not perceived as disagreeing and used judiciously, ensuring that it is in step with objectives.

Seeking clarification/information   Asking other people for further clarification or information

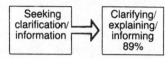

Behaviour which seeks clarification is very certain in its effect: it usually stimulates giving clarification. It is therefore a powerful shaping behaviour. But there is a complication. Again, it is basically to do with whether seeking clarification is perceived as such by the person with whom we are interacting. If it is perceived as something other than seeking clarification, obviously the behaviour shaping effects alter accordingly. Suppose, for example, seeking clarification was perceived as 'disagreeing without actually saying so'. Examples are 'So you are suggesting that we do so and so are you?' 'Tell me, what would happen if so and so occurred?' When this happens it is quite possible for disagreement to be the reaction rather than giving clarification as the behaviour shaping process predicts.

Once again we see the need to transmit behaviours that are perceived in the way in which we intend so that behaviour shaping can help in controlling the conversation. Seeking clarification is hazardous because the motives or objectives in using the behaviour can vary so much. You can seek clarification in order to become clear, to disagree without actually saying so, to get the other person to spot the snags and difficulties for himself without having to make a difficulty statement yourself, to buy time und so on. An interactively skilled person uses it to become clear and uses alternative behaviours to meet other objectives. For example, 'counselling' someone to discover the snags in their idea for themselves is more honestly and effectively done by a combination of behaviours which state difficulties and seek ideas.

Clarifying/explaining/informing   Giving information, opinions and explanations

Clarifying/ explaining/ informing	Clarifying/ explaining/ informing 42%	Seeking clarification 31%	Difficulty stating 15%	Supporting 10%

Clarifying, explaining and informing beget more clarifying, explaining and informing. The other strong possibility is that clarifying, explaining and informing will stimulate requests for more in the shape of seeking clarification. For this reason whole chunks of an interaction can be this and little else. It has a risk-free, cosy attraction about it that the other behaviours are lacking. If you seek ideas, for example, then you trigger off a chain of behaviours that may lead to commitment to some course of action. There is no such danger with clarifying, explaining and informing! The attractions of seeking and giving information, explaining things, clarifying things, repeating things ad infinitum are too tempting for many meetings and discussions. Apart from this tendency to 'loop', the data reveal no other strong trends in the wake of clarifying, explaining and informing. Difficulty stating behaviour may become apparent but it is nothing compared to the reaction to proposals.

HOW TO INFLUENCE PEOPLE'S BEHAVIOUR

The facts I have introduced in the preceding section show some strong and some less strong trends. Some behaviours are more powerful 'shapers' of other people's behaviour than others. If we list all the behaviours in descending order of their shaping prowess the table looks like this.

1st Seeking clarification	(89 per cent likely to shape clarification, explanation and information)
2nd Seeking ideas	(79 per cent likely to shape ideas)
3rd Supporting	(50 per cent likely to shape ideas)
4th = Suggesting	(42 per cent likely to shape supporting)
4th = Disagreeing	(42 per cent likely to shape clarification, explanation and information)
4th = Clarifying	(42 per cent likely to shape

explaining and informing	clarification, explanation and information)
7th Proposing	(39 per cent likely to shape difficulty stating)
8th Building	(36 per cent likely to shape seeking clarification)
9th Difficulty stating	(18 per cent likely to shape clarification, explanation and information)

It is no accident that the two seeking behaviours come out on top. It confirms the power of asking questions.

Now let us look at the data the other way round, as it were, to see what we need to do to make it as likely as possible that we elicit from the other person each of the behaviours on the list. This means scanning the data to find where the probability of each behaviour occuring is highest.

If you want the other person to seek ideas then your only real hope, and it isn't a strong one at a mere 11 per cent, is to use a difficulty statement. This sometimes exasperates the other person sufficiently to provoke them into seeking an idea from you! Apart from this, there is little you can do. Seeking ideas is one of those behaviours that the other person chooses to use or not (often not, as we shall see in the next section when looking at how frequently each of the behaviours tends to occur).

If you want the other person to propose then the best way is to seek ideas. Six times out of ten this will do the trick. Of course this says nothing about the *quality* of the consequential proposal. It might be useless, but, even if it is, having sought it you might be able to build on it.

If you want the other person to suggest then you have two rather different ways of bringing this about. Either you could seek ideas, or you could support what they were saying thus encouraging them to come up with speculative, 'off-the-top-of-the-head' ideas. It has to be admitted, however, that whichever tactic you use, you are more likely to encounter proposals than suggestions. This would not necessarily matter since, if you were using behaviour shaping as your guide, you would be careful to react to their proposals as if they were suggestions, that is, to support rather than to state difficulties.

If you want the other person to build the best thing to do is to build yourself. The data reveals building as a relatively rare behaviour (an endangered species). It rises to its highest probability at 15 per cent if you seize the initiative and start building yourself. Once again, this is an example of how behaviour breeds behaviour. Building begets building.

If you want the other person to disagree then the best way is to disagree yourself. This works in exactly the same way as building does except that your chances of shaping disagreeing behaviour are twice as good at a healthy 31 per cent.

If you want the other person to support you have two ways of going about it. Either you could build on their ideas and *make it clear you are doing so*, or you could suggest ideas, as opposed to proposing them. In both cases the likelihood of support as a reaction is quite high at 32 per cent and 42 per cent, respectively.

If you want the other person to state difficulties then the answer is to propose, as opposed to suggest, your ideas. For some reason proposing promotes statements of difficulty (39 per cent) and suggesting promotes statements of support (42 per cent). Despite this fact, most people propose their ideas by saying them as statements not questions.

If you want the other person to seek clarification/information you have a choice between two promising tactics. One is to build on their ideas with a 36 per cent probability of this stimulating seeking clarification/information. The other is to clarify, explain and inform with a 31 per cent probability of the other person asking for more of the same.

If you want the other person to clarify, explain and inform that's simple, just ask for it! Virtually nine times out of ten (89 per cent) if you ask for it, you get it.

CONDITIONS UNDER WHICH BEHAVIOUR SHAPING WORKS BEST

There are conditions under which behaviour shaping thrives. Some of them are rather obvious and are remarkably similar to the conditions under which face to face communications of any kind go well. For example, one of the requirements for behaviour shaping is that the people with whom you are interacting are listening adequately. If they do not listen then, quite clearly, the behaviour shaping effects we have just listed do not happen. Not only this but, as everyone knows, the *content* of what is being communicated also suffers. On this point it is worth adding that, whilst it is popular to think of communication problems as a *content* issue, many so called communication problems are actually confusions over behaviour rather than content. How often have you been overcome with a kind of fuzzy uncertainty about what someone is up to? You understand the content of what he says but that still leaves you ambiguous about his motives. 'Does he already know the answer and is testing me or is he genuinely seeking to know?' 'Has he deliberately left that unsaid?' 'Is he assuming that I know he knows I know?' I admit to experiencing these feelings of ambiguity quite frequently. Some senior managers are absolute masters of communication by innuendo. Even if you try to pin them down by seeking clarification they still seem able to slip out of focus and return to sentences that fade out before they are completed, *implied* suggestions and proposals and a smoke screen of other behaviours.

Another condition that seems necessary for behaviour shaping to operate successfully is that the people with whom you are interacting are sane! This may sound facetious but sanity is quite definitely a prerequisite. Perhaps one of the hallmarks of an insane person is that behaviour shaping effects cannot be observed in his reactions and that, irrespective of what behaviour is presented, he insists upon jumping off at tangents. Obviously this is an appalling over-simplification since the word 'insane' is generic and covers a whole variety of disorders. There are some people who, despite clearly transmitted behaviours, ignore them and produce unrelated reactions. Perhaps you know a few like that! Certainly they are enormously difficult to do business with!

A third condition under which behaviour shaping works best relates to the number of people involved in the interaction. Even if we are fortunate enough to be interacting with sane listeners, behaviour shaping becomes increasingly difficult in direct relation to the number of people participating in an interaction. The most favourable conditions for behaviour shaping are undoubtedly interactions between two people only. As soon as there are additional participants complications begin to set in which confuse the sequence of behaviours. I have often speculated that one of the criteria to apply in deciding whether a group is interacting as a *team* or not is to map the behaviours sequentially and, if it reads exactly as if only two people were in conversation, that would be a legitimate measure of teamwork! The confusion with most groups is that, in effect, there is more than one conversation going on in parallel. Rather like this:

Person A asks for ideas
Person B responds with a suggestion
Person C ignores B's suggestion and puts a suggestion of his own
Person A supports B's suggestion
Person B is encouraged and says his suggestion all over again
Person C is very puzzled about what happened to his suggestion and seeks clarification
Person D speaks for the first time to build on C's suggestion
Person B explains the merits of his suggestion
Person C encouraged by D building on his suggestion says *his* suggestion all over again!
and so on!

If we unravel this it is clear that persons A and B are in conversation with one another and so are persons C and D but they are having two separate and yet interspersed conversations. Add more people and even more separate conversations can break out. If group interactions like this are merely monitored sequentially without also noting the identity of the speaker, behaviour shaping effects fail to appear. It is only when the separate conversations are unravelled that the behaviour shaping effects emerge.

The final condition to be mentioned follows on directly from the previous three. It is that behaviour shaping works best when the people interacting are interactively skilful. Precisely what is meant by this is explained in Chapter 10; it suffices to say at this point that the more those interacting subscribe to the view that their behaviour is important in shaping the outcome of the interaction, and are consciously monitoring behaviour and striving to arrange it appropriately, the better behaviour shaping works. This is the corollary to the earlier points about adequate levels of listening, sanity and behaviour flagging. It reminds us that interactive skills are not an exercise in one-upmanship. The more participants are behaviourally enlightened, the more *mutual* success will be sought and achieved. This is why genuine teamwork is a rare occurrence. It requires each individual member of the team to share behavioural responsibility for its success. Most people prefer to shrug this responsibility on to the team leader by putting him 'in charge' of keeping behavioural order. If things go wrong it is his fault. In a *team*, the leader is out of a job most of the time because the individual participants are capable of ordering their own behaviour appropriately.

IMPLICATIONS OF BEHAVIOUR SHAPING

By now you should be asking 'So what?' 'What difference is this going to make?' and similar questions showing scepticism.

My answer, inevitably, takes us to the heart of the matter since behaviour shaping is at the centre of all that is involved in interactive skills. Behaviour shaping is quite literally what it's all about: the business of consciously arranging your own outward display of behaviour so that it has the desired effect on the behaviour of those with whom you are in face to face encounter. As I have said before, the whole of behavioural science pivots on the assumption that behaviour can and does occupy this central role.

Behaviour shaping therefore encapsulates all that is involved in deciding which behaviours to employ, how frequently and in what 'mix' in a given interaction. As we discovered earlier, the starting point for this decision is the situation itself closely followed by our determination to achieve an end-of-interaction objective. In some situations, armed with certain objectives, we would wish to control our behaviour so that we hang on to the shapers: whenever we are 'up against it' and wish to increase the probability of persuading others to our point of view for example; or whenever we are in a situation where the objectives of individual participants are in conflict or where we want to 'clinch' agreement to a specific course of action, to mention two more. In other situations it is perfectly acceptable to indulge in a predominance of non-seeking-responding behaviours. A classic example of when it is appropriate to do this is when you are in interaction with someone whose objectives, whilst different in detail from yours, are so similar that you can afford to fall in line behind his behaviour and still achieve the objective to which you are committed. There is no point in having a power struggle for the shapers unless your objectives are in real jeopardy.

In no sense, therefore, am I arguing that the seeking-shaping behaviours are 'good' and the non-seeking-responding behaviours are bad. It is the same old argument. There is a time and a place for all the behaviours. The situation and your objectives will tell you when and where.

Having reminded ourselves of that let us explore some of the implications of behaviour shaping in more depth.

The first implication is that we must learn to generate behaviours that are perceived in the way in which we intend if the behaviour shaping predictions are to come true. This is the old transmission and reception problem inherent in any sort of communication. Since human beings are so complicated, they will insist on processing incoming information by giving it meanings which are not always there. This is known as the perceptual process and it can play havoc with what would otherwise be 'straightforward' observations of the world about us. The only safeguard to which you, as a transmitter of a piece of behaviour, can have recourse is that of explicitly labelling or flagging your behaviour to maximize the probability that it will be received as you intended. We looked earlier at some of the everyday turns of phrase used when flagging behaviour. Quite clearly if our building behaviour say, is perceived as stating difficulties, then the behaviour shaping effects will be as for difficulty stating and not for building.

A second implication is that the more we 'mix' the behaviour categories in one piece of behaviour, the more we are likely to leave the receiver in a muddle about the bit to which he should respond. For example, if we say 'Now what ideas have you got to suggest? I was thinking it might be preferable to . . . But of course the snag with that would be . . . Or alternatively we might do so and so . . . at least that would have the advantage of . . .' we have overburdened the receiver. In general, the more we burden him with a choice the more we risk damaging the behaviour shaping effects. This argues for disciplining ourselves to arrange our behaviour in more or less single-category-at-a-time contributions. This has the spin-off merit of forcing most people to be less long-winded; but it is obviously not a guarantee because it is quite possible to prevaricate at length and still use one category. Clarifying, explaining and informing are particularly perilous from this point of view.

The final important implication is that behaviour shaping not only indicates which behaviours we should use to make it as likely as possible that we achieve the objective (Chapter 8 takes the whole issue of planning 'in step' behaviours further): it also helps us to be clear about the sort of behavioural antidotes we can use (if we must) to counterbalance the undesirable effects of other people's behaviour on us. Behaviour shaping is not a one way process and unless we monitor behaviour consciously we can get caught in the slipstream created by someone else's behaviour. This is exactly what was happening to David in the transcripts we looked at earlier (Chapter 2, pp 29–33, Chapter 3, pp 38–44.

Let me give you some examples of how it is possible to counteract the undesirable effects of other people's behaviour. In doing so they are not offered as golden rules, nor as a recipe for winning, if winning means that the others present do not achieve their own objectives. But when we are interacting with unenlightened people who are jeopardizing the achievement of mutually beneficial objectives, 'ploys' such as the following seem justified.

How to avoid being tempted into the disagreeing spiral
When someone disagrees with you, pretend to yourself that they are merely stating difficulties and not actually disagreeing. This has the advantage of making it much more likely that your response is 'constructive'. If you imagine he is stating difficulties for example, you can try to produce a suggestion or proposal to overcome the difficulty rather than be tempted into aggressively disagreeing back or defensively trying to explain the disagreement away.

How to cope with those who pathologically state difficulties
There are people who are so analytical that they predominantly state difficulties whenever they react to someone else's ideas, suggestions or proposals. It almost seems as if some deep seated principle forbids them to support or build. Such people can be useful in keeping us up to scratch by acting as a sounding board. On many occasions, however, this habit can be enormously depressing and unproductive. There are two antidotes. One puts the onus on you, the other puts the onus on them. The first is to pretend that their statement of difficulty is an invitation to build. The second is to respond by concurring with their difficulty statement and asking *them* for a suggestion/proposal. If this works, it succeeds in getting them in a proposing and you in a responding mode: a complete reversal of the state of affairs that existed previously.

How to avoid disagreeing or stating difficulties yourself
The answer is to build instead. This is not as difficult as it might seem since, if you think about it, you will realize that whenever you state difficulties you are half way to building anyway. Building is an extra thought process tacked on to a difficulty stating one. Few people seem able to build without thinking or saying their way through a difficulty statement first.

How to avoid losing control of the conversation
The best way is to hang on to your fair share of the shaping behaviours. This does not mean blatantly ignoring any of the shaping behaviours other people present to you, but it does mean disciplining yourself to finish your reply with a shaper. For example, if you are giving clarification because it has been sought, you should add, say, a suggestion so that their behaviour is shaped accordingly. A simple guideline is to finish whatever you have to say with a *question*, since we know questions are powerful shapers.

How to get people to agree with you
The answer shone through the behaviour shaping data cited earlier. The most likely way to get agreement is to put your idea forward as a suggestion rather than a proposal. Better still, if you can build on someone else's idea, support is extremely likely. You can 'arrange' building opportunities for yourself by seeking ideas and then disciplining yourself to build on the ones that come in response.

This is not a comprehensive list of behavioural antidotes. Once you start thinking in terms of behaviour categories and behaviour shaping, all sorts of other discoveries are possible.

SUMMARY

Chapter 7 has explored the concept of behaviour shaping, which was defined as the process of arranging your own outward display of behaviour so that it has the desired effect on the behaviour of those with whom you are in face to face encounters. We looked briefly at the ethics of consciously doing this and noted that interactive skill is not synonymous with one-upmanship, manipulation or the like, quite the reverse in fact.

The bulk of the chapter was spent examining the precise shaping effects of the behaviour categories introduced earlier in Chapter 5. This led us to see that some behaviours were more significant shapers than others, that sane listeners are an invaluable aid to the process and that the onus is on us to transmit really clear behaviours.

The final section of the chapter looked at some of the 'antidotes' that you can use (when you must) to protect yourself against some of the undesirable influences of other people's behaviour.

8 Non-verbal behaviour

Thus far we have concentrated on verbal behaviour with only occasional references to visual or non-verbal behaviour. In this chapter I shall redress the balance by dealing exclusively with non-verbal activity. As we shall see, verbal and non-verbal behaviour go hand in hand, often simultaneously, and both, either together or apart, have a significant impact on whether or not we achieve our objectives with people. Interestingly, there are studies which suggest that visual impact is even more important than that created by our words. 'Actions speak louder than words', is the old adage, and we shall see that non-verbal behaviours often predominate when it comes to trying to influence people. Consider, for example, what happens when people meet for the first time. Information about appearance, dress, facial expression, handshakes and bodily posture eclipse anything that might be said in those first few minutes. (This, incidentally, is one reason why it is so difficult to remember people's names. There is a tendency for people to introduce themselves and declare their name at a time when you are already suffering from 'information overload' by processing all the visual behaviours.) Even when people know each other well, non-verbal behaviours are constantly being 'read' to fathom the true meanings of what is being said and to assess whether people are on the right 'wave length'.

Non-verbal behaviour covers a range of different aspects including the following:

facial expressions
eye movements
hand movements
gestures with hands and arms
leg movements
body posture
spatial distance and orientation

There are also some fringe areas which fall into a visual rather than a verbal grouping such as dress, physique and general appearance, for example, hair style.

It seems that, without necessarily being able to describe how they do it, people make judgements and form impressions based on the non-verbal behaviours they see other people using. Most people have their pet likes and dislikes when it comes to such things as appearance and dress. Thus, people with red hair may be perceived as being volatile, people with beards as suspect, people with a short back and sides' hairstyle as organized and so on. It is more difficult to understand precisely how people form impressions based on eye movements and gestures but it happens none the less. Thus people who don't 'look you in the eye' are seen as being shifty or untrustworthy, people who point their index fingers are seen as domineering or aggressive, people who cross their arms are seen as defensive and so on. All our judgements about whether people are nice or nasty, friendly or unfriendly, confident or timid, trustworthy or untrustworthy have to be based on the behaviour they transmit and, very importantly, many of these are visual rather than verbal.

THE BENEFITS OF BEING ALERT TO NON-VERBAL BEHAVIOURS

There are two important benefits in being aware of non-verbal behaviour both in ourselves and in other people. The first is that non-verbal behaviours provide extra information that helps us to understand more completely what people are really thinking, feeling or meaning. This happens because, by and large, people find it more difficult to control their non-verbal behaviours than to choose their words carefully or even to say nothing. Non-verbal behaviours therefore, offer some useful pointers to underlying thoughts and attitudes. They tend to seep out on to the surface and act as tell-tale signs of what is happening inside.

The second benefit brings us back to ourselves and helps in our quest to be more successful in achieving objectives with people. Despite the fact that non-verbal behaviours are undoubtedly more difficult to bring under conscious control than verbal utterances, it is possible to deliberately choose non-verbal behaviours that create a favourable impression on other people. With practice you can get your non-verbal behaviour to be amenable to selection and modification and learn which non-verbal behaviours to adopt and which to avoid. There will be guidance on how to do this later in the chapter.

In summary, therefore, a heightened awareness of non-verbal behaviour has the potential to help us to be even more effective in our face to face encounters. That is the good news. There are, however, a number of problems or hazards that we need to heed if we are to be in a position to reap the benefits.

POTENTIAL HAZARDS WITH NON-VERBAL BEHAVIOURS

The first problem to be aware of is that non-verbal behaviours are easy to observe but difficult to interpret. Seeing them is perfectly straightforward since all non-verbal behaviours are, by definition, visible. The problem is inferring an accurate meaning from what has been seen. Suppose, for example, you saw someone doodling in the margin of their agenda paper during a meeting. There is a risk of interpreting this as a definite indication of boredom. However, we could be quite wrong about this since people often find doodling an aid to their concentration rather than a detraction from it. The risks of a wrong interpretation can be reduced by resisting the considerable temptation to jump to a conclusion based on the observation of isolated pieces of behaviour. It is much safer (but nothing will *guarantee* you get it right) to base an interpretation on a number of different non-verbal behaviours that fit together into a coherent pattern or cluster. So, for example, if you observed someone in a meeting doodling, looking surreptitiously at their wrist watch, stifling a yawn and gently tapping their feet this would amount to a 'cluster' of behaviours that make the conclusion that the person is bored much more likely to be true.

A second hazard is to do with generalizing. Non-verbal behaviour is one of those topics where there are more exceptions than agreements to every generalization or rule. It is therefore misleading to assume that because doodling signifies boredom in *some* people that it does so for *all* people. The dangers of generalizing apply because of the infinite variety of different people who are the product of different cultures. True, some non-verbal behaviours seem to be universal — smiling when greeting someone for example — but there are more differences than uniformities. A good example are cultural differences over body space. In the West if you wanted to establish a good working relationship with someone you had not met before, a physical distance between you and them of somewhere between two feet and four feet would be appropriate. In the Middle East, however, this distance would be considered unfriendly and impersonal. Many British businessmen have had to be warned that Arabs, in particular, find it insulting if you keep moving away to re-establish a more comfortable (by Western standards) amount of body space.

A third problem with non-verbal behaviour is not so much with the topic itself as with people's expectations of it. Some people have unrealistically high expectations of the insights it is going to yield. Non-verbal behaviour tends to be an intriguing area of study and many people have been titillated by stories of the sexual significance of such postures as crossed and uncrossed legs. If your expectations are too high then the contents of this chapter are likely to bring you down to earth with a bump. On the other hand, you might be expecting too little in which case this chapter might open your eyes to the significance of non-verbal behaviour. Many people underestimate the usefulness of non-verbal behaviour and are adamant that it is all obvious, that they knew it all already or, that it is laughably trivial. Unfortunately the subject matter is vulnerable to disparaging or dismissive comments because it often focuses on small things that at first sight appear trivial. For example, whether an interviewer nodded their head or not during an interview would seem to be an insignificant detail. In fact it makes an amazing difference to the interviewee's behaviour. The head nodding is taken as a sign of approval and encouragement and research shows that it results in the interviewee saying twice as much as would otherwise have been the case! Head nodding is therefore revealed as a small piece of behaviour that has a large impact. This is just one example among many of how it is often the little things that make all the difference.

The other reservation that people often have is one we have discussed earlier in relation to behaviour in general, namely the ethics of being manipulative. Some people feel that it is dishonest to deliberately employ non-verbal behaviours in order to influence other people. My argument remains the same: that so far as other people are concerned you are your behaviour and that, therefore, it is sensible to select behaviour that will help, rather than hinder, the achievement of objectives. This applies just as much to the non-verbal aspects of our behaviour as it does to the words we speak.

NON-VERBAL BEHAVIOUR: SOME FUNDAMENTALS

In this section we look at some of the fundamentals and in the subsequent section pinpoint some of the non-verbal behaviour patterns that help and hinder in face to face interactions.

As we have seen, non-verbal behaviour covers a whole range of visible, as opposed to spoken, behaviours. For simplicity, non-verbal behaviour is usually subdivided into just three categories.

    facial expressions and head movements
    gestures with hands and arms
    bodily posture and leg movements

These three categories are in order of importance for, not surprisingly, people tend to take most notice of the face and least notice of leg movements. Of the face, the eyes are the single most important information source and in particular where people are looking during a face to face encounter. Because of their importance, information about what the eyes are up to is always included in descriptions of non-verbal behaviour. Whether someone is looking at the other person or persons sufficiently and the amount of eye contact between them makes a significant difference to the quality of the interaction. The question immediately arises what is a 'sufficient' amount of looking and/or eye contact? The precise answer to this question will depend on the situation, of course, but to give us a useful benchmark here is some data based on two people having a rational conversation about a routine work topic. You must imagine, therefore, that the two people are not sexually attracted to each other (that would radically affect the following data) and that the topic of conversation is not emotive or especially exciting (that would also affect the data).

On average person A would look at person B for 60 per cent of the time and vice versa.

When B is talking and A is listening A would tend to look at B for 75 per cent of his/her listening time.

However, when A is talking and B is listening A would tend to look at B for 40 per cent of his/her talking time.

The typical length of a look is three seconds.

From time to time during the discussion A and B would

make eye contact. On average eye contact would amount to 30 per cent of the time, that is, half the overall looking time, and would last for one and a half seconds, that is, half the length of a look without eye contact.

These figures give us some tentative norms for what is 'sufficient' looking during an interaction. As I warned earlier, it is dangerous to generalize but many different research studies have shown that if A doesn't look at B enough, let us say for 30 per cent of the time, that is only half of the 'normal' 60 per cent, then B is likely to draw one or more of the following conclusions about A

cold
indifferent
pessimistic
cautious
defensive
immature
evasive
submissive
sensitive

If, on the other hand, A looks at B for 60 per cent of the time or more then B is likely to conclude that A is

friendly
self-confident
natural
mature
sincere
honest
open

The differences between these two lists underline the importance of looking as a behaviour. It is clear that sufficient looking helps to enhance your reputation with the other person, whereas insufficient looking tends to under-mine it. There is nothing objective or fair about this. You could, for example, be *feeling* sincere, honest and open, but if you failed to look sufficiently you would run the risk of being *perceived* as defensive and evasive. It also works the other way around: you could in actual fact be feeling defensive and evasive but by looking sufficiently the other person may mistakenly take you to be sincere, honest and open.

Another fundamental, which I have already touched on precisely because it *is* so fundamental, is the need to look for a cluster of non-verbal behaviours that seem to hang together to give a pattern. The danger of seizing on one piece of behaviour and jumping to an erroneous conclusion is very real. Earlier we illustrated this by seeing how tempting it was to assume that someone who is doodling is bored.

I cannot over-emphasize the importance of basing an interpretation on a combination of non-verbal behaviours rather than on isolated bits and pieces. Here are two more examples. Suppose you were in a meeting listening to a presentation and you noticed that the presenter was pacing around rather than standing still. What might this mean? It could perhaps indicate that the presenter was particularly anxious or nervous. On the other hand it might mean the presenter was enthusiastic and warming to his subject. Alternatively, the pacing might be a habit acquired over many years of 'thinking on your feet' and have no psychological significance whatsoever. No doubt there are more possible interpretations, indeed, it is highly likely that there are since we are speculating on just one piece of information. If I now reveal some extra data which amounts to a cluster it should narrow down the possibilities. Imagine that you notice the presenter doing all of the following things

pacing up and down
looking at the audience for at least 50 per cent of the time
speaking fast
speaking loudly
gesticulating with hands and arms
using many different facial expressions.

This now rules out the possibility that the presenter is nervous or unduly anxious. Nervous people are unlikely to look at the audience for as much as 50 per cent of the time. A much more promising interpretation is that the presenter is enthusiastic about the subject matter. Looking *in combination* with pacing, expressive gestures and speaking assertively certainly adds up to an energetic performance. It doesn't necessarily follow that you could be taken in by these signs of enthusiasm since there is more to persuading people than looking enthusiastic. But the chances are that faced with these behaviours you would conclude that the presenter was genuinely enthusiastic.

Another, slightly trickier, illustration of the wisdom of looking for clusters is as follows. Suppose you are investigating a mistake or an error that it is important to correct and as part of your investigations you interview someone who smiles whenever you ask a probing question. What might the smile mean? Again there are a host of different possibilities. The person might be smiling because he finds your questions amusing, or because he is embarrassed, or because you have reminded him of a funny story, or because he is just being friendly. If I give you a cluster of which the smiling is just one aspect the interpretation becomes much clearer. Imagine that you observe the person

    smiling
    not looking at you
    looking down at their hands
    tightly clasped hands
    no body movements
    giving clipped answers to your questions

Smiling doesn't really fit with the rest of the picture which is far from being expansive or open. The chances are you would interpret this either as a tell-tale sign of their guilt or at least as an indication that they knew more than they were prepared to say.

I shall give some more examples of different clusters and their probable interpretations at the end of this chapter. The vital point to grasp is that the best antidote for the well-known hazard of jumping to a conclusion and being wrong is to look for clusters and to be extremely wary of isolated pieces of non-verbal behaviour.

Another fundamental is to do with spatial distance and orientation. As we have already mentioned there are significant cultural differences but generally speaking the distance between you and another person is considered to be 'intimate' at distances of less than two feet. Somewhere between two feet and four feet is 'friendly' and as the distance increases beyond four feet it is increasingly impersonal. If you get too close to people you run the risk of violating their body space which people tend to find threatening. A slightly risky experiment you can conduct is to take a situation where people's body space is already being violated — say, in a crowded train or in a lift. The last thing anyone wants at this enforced 'intimate' distance is any eye contact which is in itself intimate. If, therefore, you break the unspoken convention that no-one will look at anything other than a newspaper, or the advertisements in an underground train or the floor indicators in a lift, people will find the looking, in addition to violation of body space, threatening. They, therefore, edge away from you thus leaving you more space! This is risky because as you might imagine the other possible reaction is that someone will be aggressive towards you and demand to know what you are looking at — or worse!

The orientation between you and other people in face to face interactions is another important aspect. Much research, for example, has been done on seating positions. The general finding is that people who sit directly opposite each other are more likely to fall out and argue than people who sit side by side. Side by side even though it is the most cooperative orientation is, unfortunately, not always the most convenient. A compromise is to sit at a 90 degree angle across the corner of a table or desk. This has the advantage of being both convenient and friendly/cooperative. Sitting with a desk between you and the other person is usually condemned as being unfriendly since the desk acts as a barrier. Research suggests that is it better to put the desk against a wall so that you are forced to dispense with the barrier. Another possibility is to leave the desk in a conventional position but to make a point of coming out from behind it to greet and interact with visitors. Most people perceive this as being welcoming and friendly.

NON-VERBAL BEHAVIOURS AND THEIR PROBABLE INTERPRETATIONS

The 'probable' in the title to this sub-section is there quite deliberately to emphasize the fact that there are no 100 per cent correct answers. It is always possible that someone makes a gesture or strikes a pose with no psychological significance. The clusters in this section have all been carefully researched, however, and the interpretations given are those most frequently made by the majority of people. You might like to read through the descriptions that make up a cluster and make a note of your own interpretation. The 'official' interpretations are given at the end of the chapter so that you can see how often you reach the same conclusion.

Cluster 1

Face and head
Don't look at the other person.
Avoid eye contact or immediately look away when it happens.

Hands and arms
Clench your hands.
Cross your arms.
Constantly rub an eye, nose or ear.

Body and legs
Lean away from the other person
Cross your legs
Swivel your feet towards the door

Cluster 2

Face and head
Blink your eyes frequently
Lick your lips
Keep clearing your throat

Hands and arms
Open and close your hands frequently
Put your hand over your mouth while speaking
Tug at an ear

Body and legs
Fidget in your chair
Jig your feet up and down

Cluster 3

Face and head
Stare at the other person
Have a wry 'I've heard it all before' type of smile
Raise your eyebrows in exaggerated amazement or disbelief
Look over the top of spectacles

Hands and arms
Point your finger at the other person
Thump your fist on the table
Rub the back of your neck

Body and legs
Stand while the other person remains seated
Stride around
If seated, lean right back with both hands behind your head
and your legs splayed out in front of you

Cluster 4

Face and head
Look at the other person's face
Smile
Nod your head as the other person is talking

Hands and arms
Have open hands
Hand to face occasionally
Uncrossed arms

Body and legs
Uncrossed legs
Lean forward slightly
Move closer to the other person

Cluster 5

Face and head
Look into the other person's eyes
Don't blink your eyes
Thrust your chin forward

Hands and arms
Keep hands away from your face
'Steeple' your finger tips together
If standing, have hands together behind you in an 'at ease'
position

Body and legs
If seated, lean back with legs out in front of you
If standing, keep straight
Stay still, no sudden movements, no wriggling

Cluster 6

Face and head
When listening, look at the other person for about three
quarters of the time
Tilt your head to one side slightly

Hands and arms
Hand to cheek
Slowly stoke your chin or pinch the bridge of your nose
If you wear spectacles, take them off and put an earframe
in your mouth

Body and legs
Lean forward to speak
Lean back to listen
Keep your legs still (no jiggling)

HOW TO CONTROL YOUR NON-VERBAL BEHAVIOUR

As we saw earlier, it is undoubtedly easier to control what you say than to control the visual aspects of your behaviour. However, this is *not* to say that non-verbal behaviour is automatic and beyond processes of conscious control. The secret of success is to concentrate on some simple combinations. If you do just one action in isolation, although it might be admirable as a discipline to start practising, it is unlikely to have the desired effect because, as we've seen, people gain an overall impression from combinations or clusters. So for maximum effect select just three items from each cluster, preferably one item from each sub-category that is, face and head, hands and arms, body and legs, on which to concentrate.

Of course the items you select may be mannerisms which you realize you do but want to curtail. If, for example, you realize that you often tend to

avoid eye contact
cross your arms
cross your legs

and thus run the risk of being seen as defensive you might want to practise not doing these things. On the other hand you might wish to practise gestures that you already do, more often. You might, for example, already tend to

look at the other person
have uncrossed arms
have uncrossed legs

but nonetheless want to practise doing them even more often.

The whole idea is, through increased awareness of how different non-verbal behaviour can help and hinder transactions, to force yourself to practise and thus develop skills in utilizing the more helpful clusters.

One of the difficulties you will undoubtedly experience is that of paying attention to what you are saying *and* simultaneously concentrating on your visual behaviour. Naturally the verbal and non-verbal messages need to complement each other. If what you say is out of step with your non-verbal behaviour, research indicates that people tend to believe what they see and disbelieve what they hear!

SUMMARY

In this chapter we have had an introductory look at non-verbal behaviour. The benefits of being more alert to visual behaviours were pinpointed: reading other people more accurately and using non-verbal behaviours ourselves that help rather than hinder our interactions. We have seen how it is helpful, as with verbal behaviour, to break down non-verbal activity into a number of categories covering the face and head, hands and arms, and the rest of the body.

The problems not of observing but of interpreting non-verbal behaviour were discussed with the strong recommendation that you guard against jumping too hastily to a conclusion and look instead for patterns or clusters.

The chapter contained examples of different non-verbal clusters. The 'answers' to the six clusters (that is, the interpretation most people reach) were as follows

Cluster 1   Defensive
Cluster 2   Anxious
Cluster 3   Overbearing and aggressive
Cluster 4   Friendly and co-operative
Cluster 5   Confident
Cluster 6   Thoughtful

9 How to plan behaviour

Inevitably we have already touched on behaviour planning on the way to this penultimate chapter. Let us draw the various strands together before looking more carefully at what is involved in planning and controlling behaviour.

At intervals through the book there have been hints about when and when not to plan. In general the guidance has always looked back to objectives and the circumstances of the situation in which you find yourself. I have argued that whenever you are in a face to face encounter and conscious of wishing to achieve an objective, the way you behave matters. It is under these conditions that troubling to plan, arrange and control behaviour is advisable. The actual objective may vary considerably but, in general, if you want to influence and/or impress, then conscious monitoring, planning and controlling should cut in.

There are circumstances where impressing and/or influencing are extra tough and I find it useful to have three factors particularly in mind. The first is time: the less of it or, in other words, the shorter your face to face contact, the more difficult it is to impress and/or influence. Every door to door salesman knows that. A second factor relates to objectives. When the people involved in the interaction have *conflicting* objectives it is more difficult to impress and/or influence. Every negotiator has experience of that. Thirdly, when the situation is emotionally charged with feelings running high, it is more difficult to impress and/or influence. Every husband or wife in the middle of an argument knows that.

In earlier chapters there have also been passing references to the link between the language of behaviour categories and planning itself. In Chapter 5 the point was made, but not expanded, that one of the benefits of breaking behaviour down into small 'bits', such as categories, was that it gave us a 'shorthand' when thinking about how best to behave in the light of a particular situation and desired objective. Also in Chapter 5 I was rash enough to claim that the 'secret' in actually adapting our behaviour and stretching our behavioural repertoire was to plan behaviour around behaviour categories rather than vague intentions. This chapter makes these points more convincingly and shows how to plan behaviour in the light of objectives.

WHAT IS A PLAN?

A plan, for *any* activity not just for interactions, is a detailed expression of a predetermined course of action. Some plans are predetermined well in advance of implementation; others are pieced together more hurriedly, immediately before implementation. This links back to a point made in Chapter 2 about preparatory planning and on-going planning. Preparatory planning is fine if you are lucky enough to *have* a beforehand during which to do the predetermining. On-going planning is necessary in the rough and tumble of all those interactions that 'just happen' with no, or inadequate, prior warning. Provided it is detailed, predetermined and a course of action, it is a plan. In the transcript we looked at in Chapter 5, Sheila was an example of someone who was actioning a plan she had put together *before* the meeting; Mike was an example of someone who hurriedly analysed the situation, did some on-going planning and, as it happened, went on to win the laurels as the most effective participant in the discussion! *When* we plan — whether hours or split seconds before action — does not matter. That we do so, thus disciplining our behaviour in the light of objectives, is all that matters.

Let us look at a couple of plans to see if they are detailed expressions of predetermined courses of action.

A domestic one first: suppose I notice that when my children suggest involving me in some game or another, my reaction is to decline the invitation more often than I accept it. And suppose I notice that this has a dampening effect on the children and leads to complaints from my wife. Given these conditions I may conclude that it is desirable to make a behaviour change. In order to do this I need a plan. It need not be complicated but it must be fairly detailed so that I can action it when the need arises. My plan might be:

Whenever the children suggest that I join them in playing a game I will respond by saying an unhesitating 'yes' on 100 per cent of occasions. I will follow the 'yes' up with a question about the rules/form of the game and listen to the explanation they give. If the proposed game is (a) hazardous to property and likely to lead to breakages inside or outside the house (b) hazardous to limb and likely to end in physical injury or tears, then I'll suggest enough amendments to the rules to reduce these hazards. On at least 50 per cent of occasions I must play the game *there and then* but always with an agreed time limit! On the remaining occasions I must at least have planned with the children when we are going to play the game and pinpointed *when* fairly precisely (that is, not 'sometime next week' but rather 'on Tuesday evening as soon as I get in and have read the paper for a maximum of 15 minutes'!).

The onus is now on me to stick to my plan and if I do I shall succeed in changing my 'no' reaction in these circumstances. This will please me, my children and my wife!

Here is another example of a plan, this time a work related one. It is a relatively well-known problem-solving procedure that aims to make it likely that groups of people will be able to work together and generate feasible solutions to problems. Throughout the following description of the plan the person who owns the problem and wants the participants to help him solve it is referred to as the 'client'. Another key person in the plan is called the 'leader'. He is the custodian of the procedure and ensures that participants stick to it even if they find it a strain to do so at times. In essence the plan is as follows.

1 The client states what he thinks his problem is. It is written up on a flip chart pad where everyone can read it

2 The client speaks about the problem, giving the minimum background information he believes is necessary

3 The participants ask the client questions of clarification which they feel are vital to qualify them for the next step

4 The participants are invited to restate the problem but restatement must be phrased as 'How to (do so and so)?' and are therefore positive, action orientated questions. The leader records all these verbatim on flip charts

5 The leader invites the client to pick a restatement of the problem which appeals to him as a worthwhile avenue of exploration

6 Participants are invited to give ideas and to try to build on one another's ideas in relation to the selected statement. All ideas are recorded on flip charts by the leader

7 At intervals the leader asks the client to say what he thinks is good about a listed idea. After this the leader asks him to state his concerns and doubts but always in the form 'How to (overcome such and such a difficulty)?'

8 Participants respond to these concerns by improving upon the ideas they have previously produced. Again the ideas are all recorded

9 The client is invited by the leader to say whether he sees what he regards as a possible solution. (If not then he is invited to select another statement for exploration, back to step 5 in fact — and if necessary

the workshop can loop between steps 5 and 9 for some time)

If a client believes there is a possible solution he is asked to explain what it is in his own words. They are recorded verbatim

10 The leader checks that the client believes the possible solution to be feasible and asks the client to say what his next steps will be towards implementation. The 'next steps' are recorded.

These examples should serve to show that plans are detailed, predetermined and action-oriented. These characteristics distinguish them from vaguer things called intentions. As remarked earlier, intentions have a poor track record when measured in terms of their actual translation into action. We all know what happens to new year resolutions! Resolve is not enough; we have to plan. The difference between a plan and an intention is only of degree not of kind. The difference is really one of specificity. Our new year resolutions are vague. They only state *what* we want to do and never give sufficient attention to *how* we shall manage it. A plan devotes much more time to spelling out how something shall be accomplished.

This emphasis on planning rather than intending is not new. There are plenty of examples of people actioning plans in all sorts of small ways in everyday life. Do you ever tie a knot in your handkerchief to help ensure that you will remember something? If so, that is an example of planning to remember rather than just intending to remember. Of course, the plan might not work but its existence certainly pushes up the probability of success. Do you ever compile daily or weekly 'to do' lists for yourself? If so, that again is an example of a simple behaviour plan. Have you ever written notes to yourself and left them propped up somewhere obvious — on the telephone, on a mantlepiece? 'Counting sheep' is a plan some people adopt to get them to sleep quickly. 'Counting to 10' before you speak is a plan some people use to make it more likely that they will engage their brain before opening their mouth. I once knew a manager who decided that he talked too much and didn't listen hard enough. So on certain selected occasions (*which* occasions was part of his plan) he put a bit of masking tape over his mouth. His plan was so effective in changing his behaviour that it was not long before he could dispense with the tape completely! In all these cases notice that the hallmark of a plan is its attention to detail, its specificity. Yet it is this very characteristic that often irritates people. They will complain of 'hair splitting' or of 'using a sledge hammer to crack a nut'. Changing behaviour isn't just a nut: it is a remarkable accomplishment and one which this book should help you to achieve.

BASIC STEPS INVOLVED IN CHANGING BEHAVIOUR

In a sense we are all in the behaviour change business. The essence of interacting, when there are objectives to be achieved in face to face interactions, is to use your own behaviour to influence that of others. In these circumstances behaviour change, or some people prefer the word 'modification' since it does not sound so drastic, is involved in two ways. First there is your ability to control your own behaviour in accordance with the objectives. This is, if you like, self-change. As we have already seen, changes you make to your behaviour will bring about observable changes in other people's because of the effects of behaviour 'shaping'. However, sometimes we want to change someone else's behaviour by working out a behaviour plan *together with them*. This is exactly what appraisal sessions are supposed to do, for example. In effect, we are a third party trying to encourage and help someone else to embark on self-change.

The basic ingredients for change remain the same whether we are concerned with modifying our own behaviour consciously and deliberately or with getting another person to modify theirs. In both cases the ingredients for behaviour modification seem to be:

1 The need to observe behaviour (our own and/or other

people's) with some precision leading to an awareness of what changes are necessary

2 The need to plan, again with some precision, how the behaviour will be changed

3 The need to stick to the plan by monitoring it and having feedback about its effects

Behaviour modification programmes in schools, hospitals and prisons are based on these simple principles and we need to ensure that they are embodied in our own less lavish plans.

Let us exemplify these principles by tracing them through a simple 'everyday' example. What about that maddening habit so many people seem to have of saying 'you know' at frequent intervals! Let us assume that someone else is displaying this behaviour and that we want to change it.

The first step is to *notice* the behaviour, to have observed it. Earlier we established that all behaviour is always overt and can therefore be seen and/or heard. I argued that this was an important characteristic of interactive behaviour and distinguished it clearly from, for example, underlying feelings and emotions. We can only draw inferences about them, or a less polite way of putting it is that we can only guess about the presence or otherwise of invisible things like feelings, motives and intelligence. We only have access to them via the observation of behaviour itself. So we can observe that 'you know' behaviour in a 'straightforward' manner.

The second point is less obvious and rather complicated; it harks back to our discussion in Chapter 1.

It is that we do not merely observe other people's behaviour (or anything else, for that matter) in a dispassionate, utterly accurate way: we add and subtract bits in rather an interesting manner. We use our senses (sight, hearing, smell, touch and so on) to assemble data about our surrounding environment. We do not take it all in because there is too much of it. So we select, paying close attention to some data, only taking cursory notice of other aspects and taking no notice at all of the remainder. The complication, however, concerns the way in which we process what data does come in. This is usually referred to as the perceptual process. Perceiving is not the same as seeing or hearing because the observer is active in *organizing* incoming information. We have to interpret this information, giving it meaning, slotting it against a whole store of accumulated previous experiences, checking it against our likes and dislikes. By the time we have finished, the perceptual process may have markedly distorted whatever was originally picked up by our senses. Our senses are neutral — they do not judge or assess; they just transmit as swiftly and accurately as their physiological state permits. Our perceptual processes do the rest.

There are many dramatic examples of this. We may *see* clouds in the sky but *perceive* faces or other meaningful shapes. We may see an ink blot but perceive a butterfly. We may see a labourer leaning on his shovel but perceive a lazy Irishman. We may hear someone say 'You know' at frequent intervals and perceive a pathetic person who has a limited vocabulary, or a person who is unduly anxious, or a person who clearly hasn't much intelligence, or a person who comes from a working class background — the list is endless.

The implications of this difference between the observation of behaviour and its perception are considerable. For example, it is easy to confuse our perceptual understanding of a piece of behaviour with an explanation about the causes for the behaviour. We can soon come to believe that whenever someone says 'You know' it is *caused* by some emotional state — anxiety, we might conclude. But notice that whilst it might be easy for us to believe that this is the cause, at best it is a theory — or a guess — or a convenient way of reducing the options and making us feel that we understand why people behave as they do. Most of us have built up a whole set of beliefs or assumptions against which we can slot observed behaviours with the minimum of fuss.

Another implication is that our perceptions of behaviour usually scan people themselves for explanations rather than the characteristics of different situations with which people are faced. In other words, we try to explain behaviour by attributing motives, emotions and underlying causes to people. We move rapidly from the *observation* that Joe gets through less work than Bill to conclude that Joe is lazy. From then on Joe is perceived as being in possession of a quality known as laziness. And yet, of course, Joe isn't always lazy. Sometimes he behaves in ways which, despite our biased perception of him, we would have to conclude were far from amounting to laziness: digging his allotment, for example, washing the car on a Sunday morning, playing with his children, collecting stamps.

So it can't be Joe who is lazy. It must be Joe in *certain situations* who is lazy. This means that, if anything, it is the influence of external factors in the various situations which Joe encounters that is more likely to hold the key to understanding his behaviour rather than things we might infer about Joe himself. This is a vital point because, as we have seen, when we interact with someone *we* are an important aspect of *their* external environment. Thus we are able, through our behaviour, to have a considerable *causal* influence on their behaviour.

We can check this thinking out by returning to the example of the person who says 'You know' at frequent intervals. Obviously our observation of the frequent occurrence of this piece of behaviour is a basic prerequisite before we can set about working out how to change it. Having a theory about *why* this behaviour is indulged in does not seem to be a basic prerequisite. As we have seen it might be anxiety, it might be the effects of a limited vocabulary — it might be a whole host of things. So we need to steer clear of perceiving this behaviour in that sort of way. It is enough that we perceive it as a distraction: in other words, that we find ourselves noticing the 'You knows' to such an extent that doing so ties up too many of our observational resources and we do not absorb the content of what the person is saying to us; or that we perceive it as something which irritates us, which we do not like.

How can we change it having noticed it? It is not enough to say 'I wish you'd stop saying "You know" ' all the time', or to say 'You say "You know" so often that I'm finding it a real distraction. Couldn't you cut it out?' There's clearly more to getting people to change their behaviour — even in the case of this simple example — than simply telling them to do so. This is why 'nagging' is such an uneconomic strategy for influencing change in the required direction. Wives must learn to plan if they really want to change their husband's behaviour!

What then do we need to do to influence someone to change the verbal 'You know' habit? We saw earlier that the basic steps involved observing the behaviour, planning how to change it and sticking to the plan. One approach would be to think of a way in which we can change *our* behaviour as an antidote to the other person's 'You know' habit. Behaviour shaping rears its head again. We might, for example, plan to interrupt them before they can include an unnecessary 'You know' to the end of what they are saying. Alternatively, we might try avoiding the use of open-ended questions, where we are able to exercise less control over the answer, and stick to a series of specific closed questions. This might be quite dramatic in cutting, or even abolishing, the 'You know' rate in the other person.

What, though, if we want to help the other person to help themselves in changing their behaviour? We only need one extra step. Instead of merely observing the behaviour ourselves we shall need to share our observations with the other person. This is known as 'feedback'. Feeding back involves us in finding some way of getting the other person to be as aware of the selected aspect of his behaviour as we are. It may be enough simply to tell them about it or it might be more appropriate to lead them, via questioning, to see it for themselves. So now the steps leading to behaviour change are:

1 We must observe the behaviour

2 We must feed back our observations so that the other person is as aware of the behavioural characteristic as we are

3 We must help them to plan precisely how they are going to change

4 We must leave them to stick to the plan (unless we can become an integral part of the plan itself, in which case we must stick to our bit of it too).

How might these steps be accomplished in our 'You know' example? The word 'might' should be emphasized here. There may be many alternative ways of going about it which would be equally successful. What follows is not *the* prescription for reducing or abolishing 'You know' behaviour in our colleagues, it is simply an example of a possible way.

Step 1 Observing
Monitor the conversation they are having with someone else by simply counting the number of times they say 'You know' for a timed period. Then calculate what the 'You know' rate is per minute.

Step 2 Feeding back
Then say something like: 'I hope you don't mind my saying so, but I could not help noticing how many times you said "You know" during that conversation. I reckon that on average, it comes out at roughly six "You knows" per minute'.
Let them be suitably shocked.
Say, 'Do you want to cut this rate?'
Let them say whatever they want to say.
Say, 'What impression do you think saying "You know" every ten seconds has on other people?'
Let them say whatever they want to say.
Say, 'What would be a reasonable "You know" rate in your opinion?'
Let them give you a target figure.

Step 3 Planning
Say, 'Fine, Now how are you going to get it down to that?'
Let them come up with something.
Say, 'But have you any ideas on what you can actually *do* in future to ensure success?'
Gradually build up a plan that they can adhere to in

reducing the 'You know' count to the target. The actual plan will vary from person to person but here is an example. On Mondays, Wednesdays and Fridays carry a small note book in your pocket with 'YOU KNOW' written in large letters on page one. Every time you interact get the note-book out and have it open in front of you. Whenever you catch yourself saying 'You know' put a tally mark on the page. You can soon dispense with the notebook because there aren't any 'You knows' to record!

This example of changing someone's behaviour has been deliberately simple in order to illustrate the basic steps involved. A recent article by a behaviour therapist outlined the behavioural approach to slimming. The principles were exactly the same. Painstaking attention to the behaviour of eating leading to a detailed, tailor-made behaviour plan. Just to demonstrate the similarity with behaviour plans already cited in this chapter, here is part of the slimmer's behaviour plan quoted from *New Behaviour*, 8 May 1975.

> Where meals are concerned it is essential that casual eating be eliminated by making oneself think about eating as a separate piece of behaviour not linked to anything else. Eating from one corner of a cluttered table or from a tray must be stopped. The whole table must be used and this must be cleared of everything apart from the place setting, glass, pepper, salt and so on. During the meal the slimmer's full concentration must be on the food; books, magazines and television as distractions from eating, are out. The food should be served as attractively as possible, especially if there is a reduction in helping size as part of the programme. It can also be helpful to serve smaller help-ings on a smaller plate as this tends to disguise the reduction of actual intake.
>
> During the meal the subject is encouraged to think about the taste and the texture of the food and told to put down the knife and fork between each mouthful. If eating in company he should also make conversation between mouthfuls. Before taking a drink he must ensure that his mouth is empty of food. After the meal left-over food should be thrown straight into the rubbish bin to eliminate the temptation of finishing it while clearing up. All these activities help to break previously estab-lished eating patterns. After such a piece of appropriate behav-

iour has been carried out, the subject is told to reward himself immediately by doing something pleasant from a previously agreed list of 'positive reinforcements'. It is essential that whatever reward has been chosen, going for a walk, making a 'phone call or having a cigarette, is done immediately upon completion of the behaviour.

PLANNING BEHAVIOUR IN THE LIGHT OF OBJECTIVES

It is time to link behaviour plans, be they for ourselves or for other people, to objectives. To return to the theme launched in Chapter 2 that coupled situations, objectives and behaviour together into a unified system: this can best be done by returning to the example given in Chapter 2, pp. 24–26. The end-of-interaction objective (page 25) and the behaviour plan (pp. 25–26) were described in advance of subsequent chapters that explored objectives and behaviour more thoroughly. Perhaps you can now see how it is possible to tighten up the behaviour plan by using the language of the behaviour categories. It is almost as though we need to dot the Is and cross the Ts of the plan by working out which specific bits of behaviour we must cling to in safe-guarding the objectives and actioning the plan. Planning can be envisaged at two levels: strategic and tactical. Strategies are couched in much more general terms than tactics. In this sense, the behaviour plan on pages 28–29 is strategic. It only hints at the precise behaviour categories that are vital to its implementation.

What then, would the tactical part of the plan be? And how necessary is it?

In that particular case, bearing in mind both the objective and the strategy, I feel the tactics should be:

The behaviour I will use most is seeking suggestions/ proposals. When I have to — and certainly only half as much as I seek them — I'll make suggestions myself and/ or build. I will also support and, when checking that I have recorded an idea correctly, seek clarification. I forbid myself to propose, disagree or state difficulty on this occasion.

It is by consciously arranging my behaviour at this tactical level of specificity that I simultaneously ensure that my behaviours are in step with my objective and that I discipline myself to implement the behaviour plan. This is why I claimed earlier that a detailed plan was the 'secret'.

How necessary is the tactical level? Let me put it this way: in the unlikely event of someone saying that I couldn't have both strategy and tactics as part of the behaviour plan, and that one of them had to go, I would retain tactics. I have found it entirely possible to commit myself to objectives and tactics and within those constraints to give myself room for manoeuvre and flexibility when it came to the strategy. You can test the feasibility of this to some extent by looking back at the objective on page 25 and seeing whether the main tactics just listed are obvious at that stage without referring to the strategy. Surely they are. References in the objective to 'encouraging them to come up with lots of ideas and suggestions', 'each has produced at least three suggestions' scream out for seeking suggestions as a priority behaviour. The standard about spontaneous comments on the rewarding/involving atmosphere of the meeting argues for behaviours like supporting and building and warns against proposing, disagreeing and stating difficulty. Understanding what is involved in setting an adequate objective, the shaping effects of different behaviours and the need to plan is enough.

In summary, I use behaviour categories quite literally as a guarantee that my behaviour plan will be sufficiently detailed to be actionable. It just so happens that the very same language, that of behaviour categories, is also being used to monitor, unobtrusively but consciously, the behaviours as they happen. This means that the monitoring gives instant feedback about my ability to stick to the plan and its ability to shape the behaviour of others in the direction required by the objectives. In this way the plan and the monitoring become mutually reinforcing.

What if the predetermined plan proves inappropriate? Suppose it is based on certain assumptions about the way someone will be behaving and, in the event, these are false? If you discover that the tactics you had singled out for yourself are entirely inappropriate, that is an indication that you failed to think them through adequately in relation to the objective. When this happens you should hurriedly arrive at some fresh tactics that are more contaminated by the objective than the abandoned ones were. It is much more likely that you will find your tactics redundant rather than in need of drastic revision. This frequently happens if you *assumed* that you were going to meet opposition trying to persuade someone to adopt a course of action and accordingly would arm yourself with lots of shaping behaviours. If, once the interaction starts, you find your fears were unfounded, it is merely a question of toning down your use of shapers. The need to make on the spot adjustments of this kind reinforces the importance of continuous monitoring of behaviour and conscious control so that it remains in step with objectives. It also argues for a strategy that will not straitjacket us. Hence the emphasis on objectives and tactics. In the end, where you put the emphasis in your behaviour plan, on strategy or tactics or both is a matter of personal taste. I admit to favouring tactics. Many people, however, find working through the strategy invaluable as a means of bridging the gap between where objectives leave off and tactics begin. Also, many people use the preparation of a strategy as a means of deciding on their objective. This may seem like putting the cart before the horse but a trade-off between objective and strategy can work well so long as you avoid the temptation of thinking that a strategy is an adequate replacement for an objective. Chapter 4 was at pains to distinguish between activities or plans on the one hand and objectives on the other. If this distinction is becoming hazy, it would be worth checking back through the first half of Chapter 4 and especially pages 59–63.

EXERCISES IN PRODUCING BEHAVIOUR PLANS FOR FACE TO FACE ENCOUNTERS

Chapter 4 provided six situations as part of an exercise in setting realistic objectives. We can now use those same situations and the earlier work we did on thinking out objectives as our background data for generating strategy and tactics.

Each situation, together with its objective, is repeated here to save you checking back, so that you can work out, preferably on a bit of scrap paper, what you consider to be an in step behaviour plan including both strategy and tactics. Immediately after the chapter summary I have set out my 'solutions'; once again it is important to accept that they are not offered as the 'right' answers. They are merely a basis for comparison between the plans that I think appropriate and your own work. Your strategy in particular could vary considerably and still be entirely actionable and successful in maximizing the achievement of the objective. Really wide divergence on the behaviour tactics is less likely, however. If, for example, I have planned to abstain from certain behaviours and you have elected to use them as those most appropriate to the objective, that is cause for concern. Especially since, for the purpose of this exercise, we are sharing an identical starting point in the objectives. Armed with the same objectives our tactics at least should be substantially similar.

Here are the situations together with their respective objectives. My thoughts on behaviour plans appear immediately before the chapter summary on pages 190–94.

Situation 1 Delegation problem

One of your subordinates has one real shortcoming: he will not delegate. Whenever there is any semblance of a crisis he goes in and does the job himself. When tackled on this he claims that his people respect him for being able to do a better job than they can or says that he likes 'to keep his hand in'. You suspect that his people resent these interventions whenever something is getting really interesting and regard them as a vote of no confidence in their work. Furthermore, you have noticed that this inability or unwillingness to delegate results in your subordinate taking too much on himself. He frequently stays late to 'catch up' and increasingly fails to get jobs done to deadline. You decide that you have got to tackle this problem and get him to delegate more.

Objective for situation 1
To have produced a plan with X which sorts out which of
the jobs he is currently doing himself can be given to
someone else and identifies that someone. The plan will
also include what he can do to stop intervening in a crisis.
  I shall have been successful if:

- The plan we have produced includes details on what,
  how, who, where and when
- The plan has allocated to someone else a minimum of
  four jobs which X is currently doing himself
- X has subscribed to the plan and said that it has been
  a helpful session; also that he is going to action the
  plan
- X has himself suggested that sometime in the future
  there should be a further meeting to review the success
  of the plan and to make another one if necessary
- This has been achieved within two hours.

Situation 2: Procrastinating boss
Your boss is a renowned verbal rambler and procrastinator.
You need a decision — urgently.
  In 30 minutes a very good customer prospect is due to
arrive to meet you. You have already had a series of meetings and things are looking good. Three days ago you had
a session with your boss when you asked if you might make
some concession to this prospective customer which you are
sure will clinch the deal. You didn't bother him with precise
details of the concessions you expect are necessary; you
were more interested in getting his blessing in principle with
some guidance about how much room for manoeuvre you
were permitted.
  You have already chased him twice since then for a
decision. Once he said he was still thinking about it and the
second time he was just rushing off to some meeting or
other. You are now going to see him to try to get a decision;
you predict that he will not have made his mind up and will
still be 'worrying' about it.

Objective for situation 2
To have got him to agree to all the concessions I am likely to need within 20 minutes.

I shall have been successful if I achieve this in such a way that:

- He will have shown no sign of resentment at being 'nagged' or pushed into a decision.
- He will have shared the contribution rate with me to a maximum of 50 per cent.
- He will have said that he is quite happy with the concession arrangement.

Situation 3: Taking over new departments
You have just been appointed departmental manager of a newly formed department. Your department contains three branches. One of them you know intimately having run it yourself for three years. It is now run by one of the people in that branch with whom you worked closely and successfully. The two other branches are a service branch which you never used or thought much of before and a branch selling a fairly technical product direct to the customer. You are not familiar with either the product or with operating in a customer revenue environment.

The branch from which you came is in many ways more advanced in its work than the other two. Its staff are on average higher paid, for instance, and its 'specialness' has been known to cause resentment.

You only know the two branch managers to say 'hello' to and you are anxious to get off to a good start with them both. So you have arranged to meet them, one at a time, for an initial 'getting to know each other' couple of hours.

Objective for situation 3
(For both branch managers in turn). To have produced a list of items for our next working meeting together.

I shall have been successful if:

- The list has at least six items on it, all of which genuinely require both of us

- It has been produced in not less than one and not more than two hours
- He has contributed a minimum of half the items listed himself
- The date and time for the next meeting will have been agreed between us before we break up
- He has said that he looks forward to the next meeting in such a way that I'm inclined to think he really means it.

Situation 4: The ideas woman

You have a colleague with whom you have worked on a number of projects in the past. You know her as someone who is always coming up with ideas, some good, some mediocre and some appalling. She seems to go for quantity of ideas and to let other people worry about quality. This has not earned her a very good reputation since the work 'culture' seems to put a higher premium on good ideas rather than a lot of ideas.

She has sent you a draft of a new idea she has had, worked out in enormous detail. She wants to come and discuss it with you as somebody whose views are important to her, not as somebody who will be involved in any future implementation of the idea. Unfortunately, you think the idea is completely unworkable in its present form, although you recognize there is a germ of value in it.

She respects your opinion. You hope to steer her away from making a fool of herself without losing her respect.

Objective for situation 4

To have got her to agree to a substantial rethink of her idea in order to make it workable.

I shall have been successful if:

- She has accepted that at least half of the difficulties I raise in relationship to her idea *are* genuine snags
- She has said in her own words without any prompting from me, that she now sees that the 'culture' is geared to appreciate the quality as well as the quantity of ideas
- She has told me that I've done her a big favour and

asked if she might return at some later stage to check out the modified ideas with me.

- This has been achieved in a maximum of one hour.

Situation 5: Activity diaries

You have to brief a group of your subordinates on the part they are to play in a nationwide exercise to obtain information about how they spend their working time. It involves them in keeping an activity diary each day for a month: a laborious and unrewarding task.

You are experiencing some irritation as it is not long since a similar request was made. No-one, including you, heard the outcome of the previous study and several doubted its necessity.

You have put it on the agenda of a meeting you are due to have with all your subordinates and you wonder how you can break the news of this imposed chore and get enough commitment from them at the same time.

Objective for situation 5

To have got them to identify the benefits *to us* of keeping activity diaries and to have planned how to cash in on some of those benefits.

I shall have been successful if:

- A minimum of half my subordinates have said that they agree that the benefits we have identified *are real* benefits
- Our plans do not cut across or interfere with the data head office needs from the activity records
- The plan we have produced includes the usual elements of how, who, where and when
- Our plan will not be so ambitious that actioning it is likely to interfere with work, other than the normal interruption caused by keeping an activity record accurately for one month
- I have judged that the plan, when actioned, will succeed in achieving 50 per cent of the identified benefits
- This has been achieved in a maximum of two hours

Situation 6: Salesman's expenses

You are an area sales manager appointed just six months ago. One of your best salesmen, with an extremely good record, is inclined to 'swing' quite a lot of his expenses. He is on a basic salary plus bonus system and his earnings are substantial. You were shocked by the level of these expenses from the very start but approved the claim for the first two months without querying anything with him. You knew this was sheer cowardice at the time but hoped the situation would resolve itself. It didn't and so in the third month you spoke to him about the high level of his expenses. He was sullen but agreed to watch them. Since then you have not been able to detect the slightest change.

You are about to meet him to take up the matter of expenses for the second time. You expect him to feel that his good sales record more than justifies the level of expenses and to see you as being unnecessarily petty in raising the matter again.

Objective for situation 6

To have got him to set a new standard of performance for himself which controls his level of expenses.

I shall have been successful if:

- He has set the standard, not me
- The standard he has set accords with my own ideas on a suitable level of expenses
- He has agreed that the standard will be binding for the next three months, after which he will review it
- He has said that he now sees that a 'good' salesman is not just someone who brings in sales but someone who has a feel for his revenue to cost ratio
- This has been achieved within a maximum of one and a half hours.

BEHAVIOUR PLAN FOR SITUATION 1

Strategy

My overall strategy is to get X to see the need for a plan which tackles his reluctance to delegate. I want him to feel that the work we do together in producing the plan is worthwhile so that he produces lots of ideas himself and doesn't just acquiesce.

So I'll start by asking him lots of questions about how things are going and gradually 'close in' on issues to do with him being too busy. Having got him to agree that he *is* too busy, I'll start wondering in an off-the-top-of-my-head-way, about whether something could be done about it. This way I'll slip in my idea about actually drawing up a plan which he could cling to for a while as a discipline in getting over his problem.

I'll try to get *him* to think of items for inclusion in the plan and only put forward my own ideas if he doesn't come up with those which are every bit as good as mine.

Tactics

Top behaviours on my part are seeking suggestions/ proposals and suggesting.

Second string behaviours from me are seeking clarification (particularly in the early stages of the interaction) and building.

BEHAVIOUR PLAN FOR SITUATION 2

Strategy

I'll work out in precise detail all the concessions I am likely to need *in advance* of the meeting. This is in contrast to what I did three days ago. My idea is to be as positive and as specific as I possibly can. This is to reduce the likelihood of further doubts and procrastinations from him.

I'll have to 'go at risk' during this short interaction by

referring to the prospective sale as if it has already happened and is firmly agreed.

I'll be absolutely straight with him about my objectives and the concessions I'm likely to need — not asking for anything more or less. It would not help to 'negotiate' by pitching my request higher than it need be because (a) since he is a procrastinator he won't be able to respond to this sort of treatment and won't be able to say 'no' and thus prune my request down to size; (b) I haven't the time.

I will avoid peppering my remarks with little comforters such as 'Of course, I mightn't need to go that far' since to do so will give the impression that things aren't cut and dried (and that will be like a red rag to a procrastinator).

I'm going to say everything at a comprehensible, but punchy pace.

Tactics

I'll confine my behaviour to two categories only, proposing (top behaviour by far) and seeking clarification.
The other categories are *out* — especially seeking suggestions, suggesting and building.

BEHAVIOUR PLAN FOR SITUATION 3

Strategy

To cut all social niceties and references to the past to an acceptable minimum. To start the 'real' working interaction going as soon as possible, as a means of reducing any embarrassment and of getting the interactive flow going.

I'll start by saying that I'd like the meeting to be useful to us both and has he any ideas on how we might structure it so that it is? I'll listen to what he suggests and compare it (inwardly) with the objectives I'm after. If it isn't close enough to what I want then I'll suggest mine in an involving way.

I'll spend up to 50 per cent of the available time for the meeting on agreeing its and our objectives, because this is hard work which we can both get stuck into very quickly indeed.

Once our objectives are agreed, I'll do more 'sitting back' and let him come up with most of the items for the list.

Tactics

Top behaviours: seeking suggestion, suggesting and seeking clarification. Next: building and supporting.

BEHAVIOUR PLAN FOR SITUATION 4

Strategy

In advance of arranging to see her, I'll list every difficulty I can think of in relation to her idea. I will then settle on, say, eight which, if they are to be overcome will need the idea to be completely rethought.

I'll telephone her to fix the meeting and warn her that I can see lots of difficulties so maybe I'm not going to be much use to her? This should help to ensure that she comes expecting difficulties rather than enthusiasm.

When we meet I'll ask her what she would like me to do and work her round to agreeing that I should play 'devil's advocate'. Before beginning that role I will tell her that the difficulties I'm going to concentrate on getting her agreement to were short-listed from a longer list. And I'll tell her what criterion I used in arriving at it (that these difficulties indicate a substantial re-think of the whole idea rather than a bit of tinkering here and there).

Then I'll play 'devil's advocate' according to plan.

Tactics

Top behaviours, almost to the total exclusion of all others: difficulty stating, disagreeing and seeking clarification; also some seeking suggestions.

BEHAVIOUR PLAN FOR SITUATION 5

Strategy

Since we are encumbered with this chore anyway and, since we didn't get anything out of it last time, I'm out to make sure that we do it for *us* this time, and comply with the head office request at the same time.

I'll start by 'coming clean' and tell them about the dictum. I will not grumble or refer to 'them' but just be matter of fact about it.

I'll then say ' . . . So, since we have got to do this anyway and since it involves us all in a lot of effort — as we know from last time — I wondered if it might be an idea to work out how we ourselves can benefit from all this. Can anyone think of what *we* could get out of it?' I will list the points as they come up on a big flipchart pad or blackboard which everyone can see. I will be careful to hold back from putting suggestions myself. In fact, I will only put a suggestion if (a) there aren't any coming from them at all and (b) if I can slip it in among lots of others without them noticing it came from me.

When there aren't any more ideas on benefits, I'll suggest that we see which of them we can hope to achieve by working out a plan of action. I'll start off the process by giving them the four standards I have previously set to do with the plan (my way of keeping control over the planning without actually having to shoot them down all the time). They can then work out the plan. I'll interject as necessary, but I'd rather they imposed this plan on me rather than the other way round.

Tactics

Top behaviours; seeking suggestions and seeking clarification. Back up — suggesting and building. I will be a low contributor.

BEHAVIOUR PLAN FOR SITUATION 6

Strategy

I'll start by telling him that I have been remiss in letting things slide and that I have been consistently shocked at the level of his expenses, even taking into account his excellent sales record.

I'll show him some calculations I'll have prepared expressing his expenses as a percentage of the revenue he brings in and contrast it with the percentages characteristic of his colleagues.

I'll challenge him to reduce his percentage by never talking about whether he *wants* to do it (I'll assume he doesn't) and concentrate on asking him whether he can do it. Can he still turn in the highest revenue of all the salesmen and have the lowest percentage on expenses?

I'll tell him that I would like to agree a standard with him and counsel him to be realistic since standards, once set, are apt to become a depressing liability if they are unobtainable. I'll ask him what that standard should be.

I'll help him in any way I can in the setting of the standard, other than set it for him.

Tactics

Top behaviours: proposing and suggesting (in that order). Second string: seeking suggestions.

SUMMARY

The chapter has attempted to round off its predecessors by concentrating on the mechanics of planning behaviour. Behaviour planning was hailed as the means of ensuring that behaviour is changed and modified in the desired way.

A plan, whether it be pieced together considerably or fractionally in advance of implementation, was defined as a detailed expression of a predetermined course of action. A plan is concerned with spelling out *how* something is going to be done and this distinguishes it from an intention which stops short of *how* and merely states *what*. A number of examples of different behaviour plans were given to point up their attention to detail.

The chapter then went on to look more closely at the steps involved in changing both our own and someone else's behaviour. We saw that observation, planning, monitoring and feedback were essential ingredients whether the plan was concerned with the modification of relatively 'simple' pieces of behaviour or more complex behavioural habits.

Finally, the chapter showed how the language of the behaviour categories can double as a shorthand when putting together a behaviour plan, particularly at a detailed, tactical level. The suggestion was made that objectives and tactics, provided they are precise and unambiguous enough, can 'take the strain' leaving the strategic elements of the plan more adaptable. The final conclusion was that the interplay between objective, strategy and tactics was largely a matter of personal taste provided corners were not cut on objectives and tactics, the two most specific areas, in particular.

The chapter concluded with a series of behaviour planning exercises.

10   What is interactive competence?

This is going to be a foolhardy chapter! It will spell out, in precise behavioural terms, the main hallmarks of an interactively skilled person in the hope that this will prove a useful distillation of points made in previous chapters.

I describe this venture as foolhardy because it would be so much easier to dodge this level of explicitness and thus avoid leaving myself open to protests like

'The listing of behaviours typical of an interactively skilled person reduced it all to a mechanistic level and completely missed essential characteristics like human warmth and understanding'

'Interactive competence cannot be defined: it is something you recognize when you see it but it can't be defined in cold print'

'If that is interactive skill — count me out!'

But not being completely explicit and not pinpointing what is involved in being interactively skilful, in *behavioural terms*, would be an obvious piece of hypocrisy on my part. So, risky though it is, I am going to conclude by doing it.

The main risk is the old one, encountered many times throughout this text, of failing to relate the various hallmarks to specific sets of circumstances and objectives. Obvi-

196

ously some of the hallmarks will be applicable sometimes and positively not applicable at other times. The hallmarks that follow are not, therefore, panacea-like 'golden' rules.

The hallmarks are divided into two sections. First, there are twenty attributes that you can observe *at the time* whilst in interaction with a skilful person. This is followed by five extra things that you could observe *over time*, or over a series of interactions. In neither list are the hallmarks set down in any order of importance.

Hallmarks of an interactively skilled person that can be observed during an interaction

1 He explicitly states his understanding of the objectives for the interaction and invites others present to do the same. If understandings differ, he either seeks out a compromise set of objectives that are mutually satisfactory or suggests a strategy that ensures both (or more) sets of objectives are substantially achieved. He never fobs off difficulties in matching objectives by assuming that they overlap sufficiently when they do not or by saying 'we all know what we mean'.

2 If the appropriateness of his objective is challenged he can justify it in relation to the situation and show that it is realistic and yet challenging.

3 He keeps his behaviour in step with the objectives of the interaction and does not wander off down irrelevant side tracks.

4 He explicitly labels his own behaviour whenever he considers it likely to aid its reception (which is quite often).

5 He seeks behavioural clarification whenever he is not clear how to interpret the behaviour of others.

6 He often makes overt comments on his own behaviour in relation to that of others thus showing that he is conscious of it and concerned about its effects.

7 He keeps his verbal and non-verbal behaviours in perfect accord with one another.

8 He conducts himself in such a way that you, as an observer of his behaviour, believe him to be genuine and are not suspicious of hidden ulterior motives, double dealing and the like. Even if he does not say what his objectives are, you can piece them together accurately from his behaviour.

9 He behaves in such a way that you, on the receiving end of his behaviour, feel rewarded by the encounter. He does this in a variety of ways by using your name, for example, by looking at you sufficiently, by laughing at your jokes, by showing that he has heard what you said, by expressing feelings and not just transmitting facts and by supporting or building on your ideas more often than he rejects them.

10 He 'freewheels' behind others' behaviour only when he has established that, in so doing, the objectives are being achieved adequately. In these circumstances he does not push himself to maintain control of the conversation or seek to be behaviourally the most powerful or the most 'noisy'.

11 He explicitly announces mini behaviour plans (such as 'I've been thinking about this and thought it best if I outlined my view of the problem first, then explored how yours differ before trying to think of solutions together').

12 He never produces a string of different behaviours without summarizing so that others are clear which bit(s) to react to.

13 He never acquiesces silently (because he knows that silence is a behaviour it is infuriatingly difficult for others to interpret).

14 He produces explicit suggestions and proposals that contain a possible course of action rather than an implied one.

15 He never gets into a disagreement spiral.

16 In problem solving/decision making/conflict resolving interactions he rations his 'other behaviour' (seeking and giving information, reiterating and giving clarification) to a maximum of half of all the behaviours he produces.

17 When seeking clarification he does so by testing his understanding, (that is, saying what he has understood and asked to be 'corrected') more often than in any other way.

18 He pushes for the agreement of specific action plans rather than being content with intentions.

19 When criticizing someone he is always constructive in the sense that he produces a suggestion along with every criticism.

20 When in the wrong or inadequate in some way admits it rather than pretend that he is right or adequate.

Hallmarks of an interactively skilled person that can be observed over a number of interactions

1 He is successful in achieving his objectives, either totally so that there is no discrepancy between the predicted and the actual outcome or nearly totally with only little bits of slippage here and there.

2 He makes significant modifications to his behaviour, sometimes predominantly seeking, sometimes giving, sometimes reacting, and so on.

3 He consciously arranges his behaviour whenever he is aware of wanting to achieve an objective, wishing to impress and/or influence, is in a conflict situation where objectives clash, is in a delicate situation where emotions run high and, finally, where any of the above apply *and* he is confined to a short face to face interaction.

4 He always does what he says he will do (his actions do *not* speak any louder than his words).

5 He learns from his interactive experiences by explicitly reviewing his performance in the light of his objectives and his plan and makes regular references to lessons he has learned and behaviour insights he has had.

In addition, a final hallmark could be that an interactively skilled person unhesitatingly agrees that the above criteria *do* encapsulate all that is distinctive about an interactively competent person! Even if this was not so, interactively skilled people would want to add to the list rather than reject items. I have certainly found that the interactively skilled are good at articulating criteria of the kind listed. This is not surprising since one of the consistent themes running through our scrutiny of interactive skills has been doing things consciously rather than unconsciously or unthinkingly. The correlation between behaving consciously and being able to describe the process is very high. Accordingly, I am sceptical about considering someone interactively accomplished if they are unable to articulate how they do it. I am even more sceptical about considering someone interactively competent just because they can talk about the process. If the proof of the pudding is in the eating, the proof of interactive competence is in the interacting.